To my wife Diane,
a good sport who fills my world
with love, friendship, and fun.

And to Hazel and Al,
parents who taught me the values
which make life so meaningful.

THE OPTIMIST CREED

Promise Yourself —

To be so strong that nothing can disturb your peace of mind.

To talk health, happiness and prosperity to every person you meet.

To make all your friends feel that there is something in them.

To look at the sunny side of everything and make your optimism come true.

To think only of the best, to work only for the best and to expect only the best.

To be just as enthusiastic about the success of others as you are about your own.

To forget the mistakes of the past and press on to the greater achievements of the future.

To wear a cheerful countenance at all times and give every living creature you meet a smile.

To give so much time to the improvement of yourself that you have no time to criticize others.

To be too large for worry, too noble for anger, too strong for fear, and too happy to permit the presence of trouble.

OPTIMIST INTERNATIONAL

More than 2,000
Quips & Quotes from
the World of Sports

Compiled by
GARY ALAN PRICE

Illustrated by
MIKE BEACOM

Price, Gary Alan
   Hot air

ISBN 0-920055-12-5

Layout & Typesetting by:
Pear Creative Ltd., 538 Adelaide St., London, Ontario (519)434-4744
Printed in Canada

FOREWORD

*Part of the problem in sports is that a lot
of us take it a little too seriously –*
Sportscaster Dick Schaap

Each one of us is a sports fan to some degree, or we live with a sports fan, or we work with one, or we simply know one. Therefore, this area of human endeavor we call sports affects all of us, and for the most part that effect is pleasure. Sports and the people who take part in them are meant to be enjoyed. They are recreation, they are escape, they are amusement, they are fun. They should never be taken too seriously.

More specifically, we should enjoy those things which sports personalities say. That's what "Hot Air" is all about. It's a collection of more than 2,000 quips and quotes from the world of sports. It took some seven years to compile them. The vast majority of the quotes are funny. They amuse, abuse, accuse and often confuse. They are offered for your enjoyment. In the final chapter there are some quotes which go 'a little deeper.' They speak of lifestyles, ethics and values. They are offered for your consideration.

Each quote in this book spoke to me in a special way. I hope they speak to you as well.

Before you begin, let's check the 'ground rules.' You don't have to be a sports fan to enjoy this book. It is also not necessary to recognize the speakers. The quotes stand on their own merit.

Secondly, because of the transient nature of sports, each quote is given in its original context. For example, there are several quotes from Tiger Williams. Tiger is identified by the team he played with when the words were spoken to give the quote a time frame.

Occasionally, there is some discrepancy about who actually originated a quote. In those cases, I have chosen to attribute the quote to the person from whom I first heard it.

Despite my best research efforts, it's possible that some quotes may be incorrectly attributed. Any such errors will be corrected in the future.

There is absolutely no intention in this book to embarrass anyone. On the contrary, I found each of the quotes appealing in some way and the purpose of the book is to recognize that appeal and share it. To that end I offer my sincere thanks to the people who spoke the words in this book, as well as to my media colleagues who recorded them.

I'd also like to express my deep appreciation to so many others who have made this book possible. Mike Beacom has done a masterful job of the cartoons. They add immeasurably to the fun aspects of the book. Publisher Perry D'Elia at Pear Creative in London deserves a big mention. Perry picked up the ball about a year ago and has carried it ever since. If he had not believed in this project, it would not be a reality today. My friend and slo-pitch teammate Dale Stolk has given of his time and talents by editing the book. The editor is usually the unsung hero in a project such as this and Dale is no exception. His efforts are appreciated.

Thanks, too, to the many Optimist Clubs selling "Hot Air" as a fund-raiser. All of the profits will stay in the local community to benefit the children. London Optimists Tom Dean and Fred Fickling were particularly instrumental in making this project happen. Their belief and enthusiasm definitely made a difference.

Finally, for 7 1/2 years I hosted a sports talk show on CFPL Radio in London. To the best of my knowledge, a sports show of that length in a market the size of London is unique in Canadian radio history. The people who called and the people who listened were responsible for the success and longevity of that show. Without them, there would have been no show. This book is my way of saying 'thanks' to those callers and listeners.

Yours in sports fun,

Gary Alan Price

CONTENTS

CHAPTER 1

HOCKEY PLAYERS

"The fans love us, win or tie."

Who is the greatest hockey player in the world today? No doubt many people would say Wayne Gretzky. Some might say Mario Lemieux. But who is the most quotable hockey player in the world today? That's a tougher question. The answer, though, could well be **Tiger Williams.**

Tiger is likely best remembered for his famous "done like a dinner" line but that is only one of his many quotable quotes. This particular quote followed an incident in Winnipeg after Vancouver goaltender John Garrett had blanked the Jets 3-0 for his first National Hockey League shutout. Williams decided Garrett should have a souvenir of the occasion. But what? A forward who scores a key goal can always keep the puck but a goaltender can hardly keep the net. Or can he?

Before leaving the arena that night, Williams tried to cut a piece of mesh from one of the nets. However, security guards caught him in the act and sent him away empty-handed.

Muttered a miffed Tiger: "I guess nets cost too much in Winnipeg."

Montreal Canadiens defenceman **Larry Robinson:**
"Proper breathing techniques are very important to a hockey player. I never leave home without mine."

New York Islanders goaltender **Chico Resch:**
"Playing hockey is the only job I know of where you get paid to take a nap on the day of a game."

King Clancy, *describing Gordie Howe's elbows:*
"Like windshield wipers, always up and in your kisser."

Los Angeles Kings forward **Charlie Simmer**, *after a particularly boring game:*

> "Was that a lousy game or what? It was the kind of game in which players on both teams gain weight."

New York Islanders forward **Anders Kallur,** *about some trade rumors:*

> "I don't care if they trade me. I just hope they wait until after the pre-game meal in St. Louis. We always have such great pre-game meals in St. Louis."

Toronto Maple Leafs defenceman **Jim McKenny**, *on how to handle Gilbert Perreault of the Buffalo Sabres:*

> "I always rushed him at his own blue line. That way, I wasn't the last guy to get beat."

Sportswriter **Dick Trust**, *after the left wing of the plane carrying the Boston Bruins hit a bus in a minor accident at Los Angeles Airport :*

> "The Bruins problems at left wing continue."

Philadelphia Flyers centre **Bobby Clarke:**

> "My dad always told me you never get anything for nothing, and I really believe that."

Ann Carpenter, *about her son Bobby after he broke into the NHL:*

> "Two months ago, he left home looking like a handsome young man bound for college. Now his face is covered with stitches and he looks more like Terry O'Reilly."

Chicago Blackhawks goaltender **Glenn Hall:**

> "I love the travel, the card games, the bull sessions. In fact, I love everything about hockey but the games."

London Knights centre **David Simpson:**

> "I can't skate very well, I don't make great plays, I can't shoot, I don't like to go into the corners, I can't hit and everyone knows I can't fight. All I can do is think. And even at that, I don't start to think until I get the puck."

Philadelphia Flyers bad guy **Dave Schultz:**

> "I believe in fighting a guy one-on-one. But nobody's allowed to hit the Flyers in their own building. If you do, Freddie Shero sends out one of his goons."

Montreal Canadiens forward **Steve Shutt:**

> "The fans in Montreal love us, win or tie."

Calgary Flames centre **Dan Quinn,** *on the way teammate Charlie Bourgeois dresses:*

> "Charlie Bourgeois couldn't dress a turkey."

Bobby Orr, *on his bad knees:*

> "If I were a horse, they'd probably shoot me."

Minnesota North Stars goaltender **Don Beaupre,** *when asked if being only 5'8" and 150 pounds created a problem:*

> "I just have to stop the puck, not beat it up."

Gordie Howe, *on charges that he was a dirty player:*

> "Naw, I wouldn't call myself dirty, just hyper-aggressive from time to time."

Toronto Maple Leafs defenceman **Pat Ribble,** *after he was acquired from Chicago following a brief stint with the Blackhawks:*

> "I guess my Chicago scrapbook will be a short one."

Bobby Hull, *on Toronto Maple Leafs owner Harold Ballard:*

> "The only way to get Ballard's attention is to hit him in the face with a spade."

Don Maloney *of the New York Rangers, talking about his New Year's resolution:*

> "I promised myself I'd get as many goals this year as Wayne Gretzky got last week."

Washington Capitals defenceman **Yvan Labre,** *after he took a beating in a hockey fight:*

> "My problem was that my arms are too short. If my arms had been longer, I would have creamed that guy."

Bobby Clarke, *after his retirement as a Philadelphia Flyer:*

> "There was nothing about the game I didn't like, except getting older, and I couldn't figure out how not to."

Toronto Maple Leafs goaltender **Turk Broda,** *trying to explain why he always played so well in the playoffs:*

> "There are two possible explanations. Either I needed the bonus money to pay the bills, or I was too dumb to feel the pressure."

Philadelphia Flyers forward **Brian Propp,** *on the disadvantage of wearing a protective visor:*

> "The only bad thing is when I yell at the ref, it rings in my ears."

Chicago Blackhawks centre **Stan Mikita,** *on his favorite shot:*

> "Anything that's six inches in front of an open net."

Fringe hockey player **Tim Butler,** *after trying to make the Mohawk Valley Stars of the Eastern League:*

> "I tried hard. I was the first guy at practice every day and the last guy to leave. My problem was that I was too consistent. I did the same thing with the team parties."

Los Angeles Kings goaltender **Gary Simmons,** *on why he bought a saddle when he did not own a horse:*

> "This way I'll be ready if I ever get one."

New York Rangers goaltender **Glen Hanlon,** *when asked at what age a youngster should start learning the position:*

> "Eight weeks is a great time. Stick him in a goal and roll some things at him."

Philadelphia Flyers forward **Rick MacLeish,** *after suffering a severe cut across his throat:*

> "I knew I had a problem when I took a puff of a cigarette and smoke came out of my neck."

New York Rangers forward **Pierre Larouche,** *when asked the best thing about being recalled from the minors:*

> "Shorter runways. Buses have a hard time taking off on short runways."

4

Toronto Maple Leafs centre **Darryl Sittler,** *after his 10-point game against Boston:*

> "I understand their goaltender went out and tried to commit suicide by jumping on some railroad tracks but the train went between his legs."

Edmonton Oilers goaltender **Andy Moog,** *after teammate Wayne Gretzky was hit with a heavy bodycheck:*

> "Gretz said he saw stars. He must have meant Morgan Fairchild."

Gordie Howe:

> "You can't play hockey and think about getting hurt. Once you start thinking about it, that's when you do get hurt."

Tiger Williams:

> "I don't know why Denis Potvin thinks he's so smart. He ain't any more one of them inteffectuals than any of the rest of us."

Czechoslovakian defector **Miroslav Ihnacak,** *after playing his first game in the small Buffalo Memorial Auditorium:*

> "It was like being in a butcher shop back home, elbowing your way for the good cuts of meat."

U.S. Olympic goaltender **Jim Craig,** *while being honored at Boston University for his part in the American gold medal performance at Lake Placid:*

> "Do I still have to pay the $500 worth of parking tickets I got here as a student?"

Laurie Boschman, *in awe of his surroundings when he broke in with the Toronto Maple Leafs:*

> "When I walked in, there were even skate laces waiting for us if we needed them."

Montreal Canadiens defenceman **Serge Savard,** *on teammate Guy Lafleur:*

> "Lafleur is the best. He was made for this game."

Mike Palmateer, *when he joined the Toronto Maple Leafs:*

> "Your hunt for a goaltender is over."

Boston Bruins forward **Rick Middleton,** *during his recovery from shoulder surgery:*

> "I can shoot and I can follow through. I can do just about anything I want to. I can even pick up dinner cheques, as long as they're not too heavy."

Former NHL player **Gerry James,** *downplaying the violence in hockey:*

> "A punch in the mouth never hurt anyone."

Edmonton Oilers defenceman **Randy Gregg,** *talking about his first NHL goal:*

> "It was in Winnipeg in 1982. I took a weak wrist shot from the blue line. There was a scramble in front of the net and the puck went in the corner. It felt good but I'm amazed that I remember it."

Derek Sanderson, *talking about his problems with the bottle:*

> "I threw a party in 1973 and it lasted till '77."

Gordie Howe, *when asked if he thought Reggie Fleming was a hard-nosed player:*

> "I don't know. I've never felt his nose."

Toronto Maple Leafs forward **Wendel Clark:**

> "Hockey is like growing crops. You put your crop in, you work the land as hard as you can and if the crop fails you can't look at yourself as a failure because you've done your full share."

Former New York Rangers goaltender **Ken McAuley,** *talking about a game in which his team lost 15-0 to Detroit:*

> "The Red Wings were in our zone for so long that at the end of the period there was no need to clean the ice at the other end."

Edmonton Oilers forward **Kevin McClelland,** *on taking part in a Superstars competition with a football player, a skier, and others:*

> "I'll be all right as long as I don't have to stickhandle."

Former NHL player **Pierre Bouchard,** *when asked if he might get back into the league:*

> "Only if I learn to play the organ."

WAYNE GRETZKY, TAKING A POKE AT HIMSELF:

"THERE'S A NEW WAYNE GRETZKY
DOLL ON THE MARKET. IT ONLY CRIES
WHEN IT GETS HIT."

Bobby Clarke, *describing the play of the Philadelphia Flyers:*

"We take the shortest route to the puck and we arrive in ill humor."

Quebec Nordiques defenceman **Pat Price,** *on his team's intense rivalry with the Montreal Canadiens:*

"It's gotten to the point where someone could get hurt. They hate blue, we hate red, and it goes from there."

Former New York Rangers forward **Rod Gilbert,** *on hockey fights:*

"If hockey fights were fixed, I'd have been in more of them."

Jacques Plante, *describing the pressures of being an NHL goaltender:*

"How would you like it if you were in your office and you made a little mistake, and then suddenly a bright red light flashed on behind you and 18,000 people started screaming 'Pig! Stupid! You couldn't even stop a basketball. Get the bum out of there?' "

Gordie Howe, *on the general-managerial abilities of his wife Colleen:*

"All I know is that she has 'general-managed' me pretty well for years."

Edmonton Oilers forward **Mark Messier,** *when asked for a good rumor about Wayne Gretzky:*

"I've never heard one.

Former NHLer **Bill Clement,** *assessing his career:*

"If the rink didn't have boards, I'd have been great."

Lisa Dionne, *talking to a friend about her hockey-playing father Marcel:*

"There's my dad. Look at his scars."

St. Louis Blues defenceman **Bob Plager,** *on a race he had with an equally-slow skater:*

"It wasn't a photo finish, it was an oil painting."

New York Rangers equipment man **Joe Murphy,** *explaining how he can tell if a game has been a tough one:*

> "By the number of socks I have to sew. Usually I sew 15 to 18. Following the opening playoff game with Philadelphia I had to sew all 40. It means everyone was going into the corners and getting ripped by skates and sticks."

Former NHL goaltender **John Davidson,** *on the best thing about retirement:*

> "No curfews."

Philadelphia Flyers centre **Ken Linseman,** *after some opponents accused him of being crazy:*

> "I'm not crazy. I stay away from Billy Smith. He's crazy."

Montreal Canadiens forward **Rejean Houle,** *after growing a beard:*

> "When you play for the Canadiens and you don't win the Stanley Cup, you want to hide behind something."

Vancouver Canucks goaltender **Richard Brodeur,** *when asked what Wayne Gretzky does best:*

> "Make you look bad."

Gordie Howe *of the New England Whalers, on his possible retirement:*

> "I'll just retire at 65 like everybody else."

Tiger Williams:

> "Nice guys finish last. I'd rather play with a bunch of bleeping jerks."

Boston mayor **Kevin White,** *on Bobby Orr:*

> "Bobby Orr has been to Boston the equivalent of a great natural or historical resource, like Paul Revere's house or the Bunker Hill Monument. Some things cannot be replaced."

Comedian **Bob Hope,** *at an NHL luncheon:*

> "I feel right at home here among all these hockey players. Of course, I've always enjoyed entertaining the fighting men."

Edmonton Oilers winger **Pat Hughes,** *after he went six weeks without scoring a goal:*

> "I'd get a penalty every so often just so my mother would know I was still playing."

Chico Resch, *on his talkative nature:*

> "If I wasn't talking, I wouldn't know what to say."

Former Toronto Maple Leafs defenceman **Carl Brewer:**

> "John Ferguson of Montreal was the ultimate goon but I wouldn't say it to his face."

Gordie Howe, *giving some advice to Wayne Gretzky when Wayne broke into the NHL:*

> "You've got two eyes and one mouth. If you keep two open and one closed, you'll learn a lot."

Boston Bruins forward **Terry O'Reilly,** *on his skating style:*

> "Guy Lafleur flies down the ice. Steve Shutt soars. Bob Gainey barrels. I just sort of crash."

New York newspaper columnist **Dick Young:**

> "Islanders goaltender Billy Smith has the nerves of the Berlin Wall."

Defenceman **Gaston Gingras,** *after he joined the Montreal Canadiens:*

> "There's something special here. I think it's in the sweater."

Turk Broda, *after he retired as Toronto Maple Leafs goaltender:*

> "The only sign I had that I was getting older was when the butterflies in my gut slowed up."

Bobby Clarke:

> "The greatest thing I found as a professional athlete was when you had everybody on the team pulling for the same common goal and then accomplishing that. For me, that's the greatest feeling. The Stanley Cups were the ultimate. They were like a dreamland."

10

Pat Daley, *after he scored a goal on his very first shift in the NHL:*

> "Everything just lit up for me."

Sportswriter **Frank Orr:**

> "If the Hunter family (with NHLers Dave, Dale and Mark) ever has a family feud, it will last three weeks and no prisoners will be taken."

Derek Sanderson, *on his battle with the bottle:*

> "I'm much happier now — poor, crippled and sober — than I ever was rich, healthy and drunk."

Detroit Red Wings forward **Gordie Howe,** *to Toronto Maple Leafs goalie Johnny Bower, after a shot which looked like a sure goal hit Howe in the crease:*

> "Hey, John, I just made a leg save for you."

Hall of Famer **Bill Chadwick,** *on Bobby Orr:*

> "He is the best I have ever seen. It's a long drop down to the best of the rest."

Tiger Williams:

> "I'm better than Bobby Orr because I try harder."

Sportswriter **John Herbert,** *about a certain junior team's pre-game strategy:*

> "They always stop at a gas station on the way to the game so they can pump up a few heads."

Montreal Canadiens goaltender **Jacques Plante,** *when asked why he never got involved in fights:*

> "It's not in my contract."

Dave Lewis *of the New York Islanders, talking about the speed of his slapshot:*

> "Some guys skate faster than my shot."

London Knights centre **David Simpson:**

> "I started my hockey career as a goaltender, then moved to defence and then to the wings. They finally put me at centre because that's where I hurt the team least."

Bobby Hull, *after scoring his 1,000th career goal:*

"It's nice but really the 1,000th goal was just like any other."

Philadelphia Flyers forward **Gary Dornhoefer,** *after he was sent out to 'watch' Montreal's Guy Lafleur:*

"I watched him score two goals, coach. Wasn't he terrific?"

Kingston Canadians defenceman **Todd Clarke,** *about his former coach who did not like physical hockey:*

"Maybe he's going to grow flowers around the rink, too."

Bobby Orr, *on Wayne Gretzky:*

"He's the greatest player I've ever seen in my life."

Stan Jonathan *of the Boston Bruins, at a celebrity roast for teammate Wayne Cashman:*

"It's been a while since anyone from my tribe roasted a white man."

Philadelphia Flyers defenceman **Frank Bathe:**

"The ice was really chippy out there tonight. Now guys like Mark Howe know how I feel every night."

New York Rangers defenceman **Steve Richmond,** *after being called up from the minors:*

"You're probably a piece of meat everywhere you play but at least in the NHL you're prime rib."

Gordie Howe, *when asked at the age of 51 how many more years he could play:*

"I've got it down to days."

Los Angeles Kings defenceman **Mark Hardy,** *explaining why he changed his number from 20 to 25:*

"I don't want any more zeroes in my life."

Former NHL great **Fred 'Cyclone' Taylor:**

"Good hockey should be a game of speed, stick-handling and skating. If they want violence, they should go to the wrestling matches."

Larry Robinson, *on his reluctance to give blood:*

"The last time I gave, they found three olives in it."

Tiger Williams, *before an exhibition game against a team from the Soviet Union:*

"I haven't decided yet whether to use my nuclear stick or my Star Wars model."

St. Louis Blues goaltender **Rick Wamsley,** *on the advantages of having Jacques Plante as goalie coach:*

"It's like being able to go to a library and take out every book ever written about playing goal."

New Jersey's **Bob Hoffmeyer,** *explaining his retirement:*

"I figure I've seen enough hockey because I was always so far behind the play that I got a good look at everything."

Bobby Hull, *discussing the state of the WHA:*

"For every team that has improved, four are worse."

Atlanta Flames forward **Curt Bennett,** *talking about a recent hockey fight:*

"I just punched him. I didn't do anything un-American."

Chico Resch, *when asked to name the biggest weakness of Soviet goaltender Vladislav Tretiak:*

"Vodka."

Sportswriter **John Herbert,** *about the aggressive play of a certain Junior 'A' team:*

"They ought to send these guys to the Middle East as a peace-keeping force."

Bobby Clarke:

"The worst thing in the world is to wake up in the morning and have nothing to do."

Mark Howe, *after a fan told him he wasn't as good as his father Gordie:*

"Who was?"

New York Islanders goaltender **Billy Smith:**

> "Missing the playoffs in the NHL is like having your name left out of the telephone book."

U.S. President **Ronald Reagan,** *at a luncheon before the NHL all-star game in Washington:*

> "I understand the Washington Capitals are going to trade for Wayne Gretzky. They only have to give up two first-round draft picks and the state of Texas."

CHAPTER 2

HOCKEY COACHES

"I have nothing to say. Any questions?"

As coach of the New York Rangers, **Herb Brooks** was known for his honesty and humor, especially in assessing his own team. This was one of those assessments.

"Our goaltending has been okay recently but really nothing to write home about. The defensive play hasn't been anything to write home about either. In fact, if you're going to write home, ask for money and cookies."

Vancouver Canucks coach **Harry Neale:**

"We're losing at home and we're losing on the road. My failure as a coach is that I can't think of anywhere else to play."

Toronto Maple Leafs coach **Roger Neilson,** *explaining why he selected Tiger Williams to serve a bench penalty:*

"Tiger has the most experience."

Detroit Red Wings general manager, **Jim Devellano,** *commenting on certain trade rumors:*

"That's totally wrong. If it were true, I'd lead my own lynching."

Philadelphia Flyers coach **Fred Shero:**

"Life is just a place we spend time between games."

North Bay Centennials coach **Bert Templeton,** *after a particularly bad game:*

"If that's the way I've taught my team to play hockey, I've got a lot to learn about the game."

Minnesota North Stars coach **Glen Sonmor,** *after a game dominated by Wayne Gretzky:*

> "What Wayne Gretzky did is the most unheard-of thing I ever heard of."

Herb Brooks, *after he accepted the coaching job with the New York Rangers, a team which had not won a Stanley Cup in 41 years:*

> "If I'm not part of a Stanley Cup winner within the next 41 years, I'll gladly resign."

Vancouver Canucks coach **Phil Maloney,** *when he was approached by reporters after a bad loss:*

> "After a performance like that, who would want to talk to me?"

Montreal Canadiens coach **Scotty Bowman:**

> "A winning atmosphere is the biggest thing in sports."

Toronto Maple Leafs owner **Harold Ballard,** *about one of his team's unbeaten streaks:*

> "Church ain't over until the choir stops singing."

Gerry Cheevers, *after he was named coach of the Boston Bruins:*

> "I may have just taken the biggest pay cut in hockey history but I wouldn't want to coach any other team, except maybe the New York Yankees."

London Knights coach **Bill Long,** *when asked for his thoughts prior to a big game:*

> "I never think, it hurts the club."

New Jersey Devils coach **Tom McVie:**

> "My wife says I love hockey more than her. That's true. But I do love her more than baseball."

Hartford Whalers coach **Jack Evans,** *after a reporter said he wanted to feature him in a 'personality piece':*

> "I didn't know I had one."

Montreal Canadiens coach **Toe Blake,** *when asked for a prediction on an upcoming playoff series:*

> "Predictions are for gypsies."

Vancouver Canucks coach **Harry Neale,** *when asked why his team was not higher in the standings:*

> "I don't know. If you can figure it out, call me back in 30 minutes. There might be a place for you in the organization."

NHL president **John Ziegler,** *after a successful luncheon at the White House before the league all-star game:*

> "I had a tough time sleeping the night before the luncheon. I kept dreaming about breaking the china."

Minnesota North Stars general manager **Lou Nanne:**

> "Some people say anything's possible. Have they ever tried skiing through a revolving door?"

New York Rangers coach **Herb Brooks,** *on Reijo Ruotsalainen:*

> "Trying to have him play like everyone else would be like having Picasso paint my garage."

Toronto Maple Leafs general manager **Punch Imlach,** *on charges that he did not communicate with the players:*

> "I learned one thing in the army. The generals don't hang around or talk to the privates."

Winnipeg Jets coach **Barry Long,** *after a lop-sided loss:*

> "I never considered changing goaltenders but I did consider putting them both in at once."

Anonymous observer, about Roger Neilson:

> "Roger is so hockey crazy that he draws faceoff circles on his ice cubes."

Oshawa Generals general manager **Sherry Bassin**

> "In Africa, they call them cannibals. In Canada, we call them sports reporters."

Fred Shero's wife,when asked if Fred picked up all of his deep, motivational messages from reading:

> "What reading? He gets those sayings on the little cards in the tea boxes we buy."

17

NHL president **Clarence Campbell:**

> "Hockey is a violent game. If it isn't violent, it isn't hockey."

Minnesota North Stars coach **Glen Sonmor,** *assessing the careers of some players:*

> "They go from crushers to rushers to ushers."

Craig Patrick, *an assistant coach of the American hockey team at the Lake Placid Olympics in 1980, just before the final game:*

> "We can't make any mistakes tonight. This is for all the money...well, not the money, all the glory."

Vancouver Canucks coach **Bill Laforge:**

> "Luck is what happens when preparation meets opportunity."

Los Angeles Kings coach **Don Perry,** *on his team's chances going into a certain season:*

> "We're going to have to give 100 per cent and maybe get some help from the guy upstairs. And when I say the guy upstairs, I don't mean (general manager) George Maguire."

London Knights coach **Paul McIntosh,** *about a new addition to the team:*

> "I love him. He's crazy. He's got a tattoo and everything."

Herb Brooks:

> "I'm so edgy on game days I even snap at my dog and I don't have a dog."

Birmingham Bulls coach **John Brophy,** *after the club folded:*

> "I thought I saw some light at the end of the tunnel. I didn't know it was a train coming."

Boston Bruins coach **Gerry Cheevers,** *after Ken Linseman set up a goal by Charlie Simmer:*

> "That's a play we couldn't have made last year. Linseman was in Edmonton, and Simmer was in Los Angeles, and Kenny would have had to pass it through the Rockies to get it to him."

HAROLD BALLARD: "SOME OF MY PLAYERS GO INTO THE CORNERS LIKE THEY HAVE POCKETS FULL OF EGGS."

Harry Neale, *explaining the first move he plans to make when he takes over as general manager of the Vancouver Canucks:*

> "I'm going to draft the Stastny's old man and the father of the Sutters and start a breeding farm. Those are pretty good bloodlines."

Toronto Maple Leafs owner **Harold Ballard,** *following his firing and rehiring of coach Roger Neilson:*

> "It was all a hoax. He wasn't fired, he was just put on furlough for a day or two."

Toronto Maple Leafs coach **Roger Neilson,** *following his infamous firing and rehiring:*

> "Yesterday, if you had told me this was possible, I would have said the whole thing was crazy."

Edmonton Oilers assistant coach **John Muckler,** *after defenceman Larry Melnyk scored his first goal in 140 games:*

> "Well, there goes another defensive defenceman."

Colorado Rockies coach **Aldo Guidolin,** *when asked if he were having nightmares because of his club's poor record:*

> "I can't have nightmares because I can't sleep. I'd have to rally to have a nightmare."

Washington Capitals general manager **Milt Schmidt,** *during the club's dismal first season:*

> "If we avoid injurics and play up to our potential, we can still finish last."

King Clancy, *putting hockey into perspective:*

> "If you don't have fun, what's the sense of playing?"

Minor hockey coach **Don Wilson,** *encouraging his young players to do their best regardless of the outcome:*

> "You win some and you lose some but you dress for 'em all."

Boston Bruins coach **Don Cherry:**

> "When I went into the parking lot after practice the other day, the players were getting into Mark IVs and a new Corvette. Me? I got into my old Chevy Monte Carlo."

North Bay Centennials coach **Bert Templeton,** *after his team had been shut out two games in a row:*

> "It's our new strategy. We want to confuse the other teams so they won't know who to send their checking lines out against."

Boston Bruins general manager **Harry Sinden,** *talking about the quality of leadership:*

> "This thing we're talking about is a tangible intangible."

Maple Leaf Gardens public relations director **Stan Obodiac:**

> "I shudder to think what would have happened to the Canadian World War II effort if we had depended on track and swimming participants instead of mannish hockey players."

Cornwall Royals coach **Orval Tessier,** *to 130-pound Dan Daoust when he arrived at training camp:*

> "I don't need another leg for the kitchen table."

Los Angeles Kings coach **Parker MacDonald,** *explaining what it's like to cover Wayne Gretzky during a power play:*

> "It's like trying to throw a blanket over a ghost."

Edmonton Oilers assistant coach **Bob McCammon,** *as he put on some aftershave lotion following a tough loss:*

> "Any more games like tonight and I'll be drinking this stuff."

Toronto Maple Leafs coach **Punch Imlach,** *about young Rogie Vachon, who was brought up from the minors by Montreal just before the playoffs:*

> "He's nothing more than a Junior 'B' goaltender."

New York Rangers coach **Herb Brooks,** *a former insurance salesman, after a tough playoff game:*

> "I told my wife to renew my insurance licence."

Vancouver Canucks coach **Harry Neale,** *on goaltenders:*

> "They spend all of practice trying not to get hit by the pucks, then all of the game trying to get hit by the pucks. It's a stupid job."

Detroit Red Wings general manager, **Jim Devellano,** *explaining what it's like to challenge for a playoff spot in a weak division:*

"It's a lot like puppy love. Nobody else takes it seriously but it's real to the puppies."

Winnipeg Jets coach **Tom McVie,** *assessing his team's problems:*

"It's like in the old Western films where the Indians are circling the fort and the cavalry comes to the rescue. Well, the cavalry ain't coming here, this is it. Every time you try to make a deal with a general manager in this league, they give you snow in the winter, and if you're drowning they throw you an anchor."

Bob Plager *of the St. Louis Blues, talking about Chicago Blackhawks coach Bob Pulford:*

"A bar in Chicago asked Pulford to leave so they could start happy hour."

Toronto Maple Leafs coach **Red Kelly,** *advocating 'pyramid power' in a playoff series against Philadelphia:*

"It's our pyramid power against Kate Smith's mystic power."

NHL great **Bobby Hull,** *on the calibre of hockey coaching:*

"Some coaches couldn't coach a dog out of a storm with a T-bone steak."

St. Louis Blues coach **Red Berenson,** *trying to describe the plight of the hockey coach:*

"Imagine yourself sitting there and a fire breaks out. Nobody can move except a handful of guys and you've got to tell them how to put out the fire. You've got to tell them what to do, how to do it, where to do it and why they have to do it. You have to convince them that they can do it. And you have to tell them that if they don't do it, it's your butt that's gonna get burned. Maybe that's where the term 'firing the coach' started."

Harry Neale:

"I know my players don't like my practices but that's okay because I don't like their games."

New York Islanders coach **Al Arbour,** *when the NHL was considering a franchise in Saskatoon:*

> "Harold Ballard claims the only way to get to Saskatoon is by dogsled. His real worry is finding two dogs willing to take him."

Fred Shero:

> "I guess the one thing I've learned from sports is that we can't get along in life without each other. We need each other. That's why people get married."

Colorado Rockies president **Armand Pohan,** *when he hired coach Billy MacMillan to replace Don Cherry:*

> "He has a big pair of lungs to fill."

Herb Brooks, *explaining why he left the bench to watch a game from the press box:*

> "I heard they had great hot dogs up there so I decided to try one. Do I have mustard on my chin?"

Los Angeles Kings coach **Bob Berry:**

> "My best move was bringing Charlie Simmer up from the minors. My worst move was sending him there in the first place."

Hartford Whalers coach **Jack Evans:**

> "A hockey team is like a bird. If you hold your hand open, it might fly away. If you hold it too tightly, you might kill it. All you can do is cup it softly and hope it doesn't poop in your hand."

New York Rangers coach **Phil Watson,** *at a news conference following a bad game:*

> "Gentlemen, I have nothing to say. Any questions?"

Montreal Canadiens coach **Scotty Bowman:**

> "Hard work wins more games than anything. You've got to get team dedication."

Minnesota North Stars coach **Glen Sonmor,** *when asked what it took to be an NHL coach:*

> "Good luggage."

23

New York Rangers publicist **John Halligan:**

> "Next season, Wayne Gretzky might lead the NBA in scoring."

Toronto Toros coach **Bobby Baun,** *after his team played a particularly bad game:*

> "If I could, I'd throw up on all of them."

Maple Leaf Gardens owner **Harold Ballard,** *after the Gondola used for so many years by Foster Hewitt was torn down and burned:*

> "Hell, we're not in the historical business and that Gondola wasn't so old anyway."

Roger Neilson, *as coach of the Buffalo Sabres following his tenure in Toronto:*

> "It's easier here in Buffalo. In Toronto you were on your own."

Vancouver Canucks coach **Harry Neale,** *after a 7-6 win over Pittsburgh:*

> "Did anybody get hurt, besides the goal judge?"

Philadelphia Flyers coach **Fred Shero,** *after he coached the club for the 500th game:*

> "Just because you've been with one team for a long time is nothing to be proud of, especially if you could have done a better job."

Hamilton Fincups coach **Bert Templeton,** *on playing the London Knights, whose rink is next door to a supermarket:*

> "London is the only city in the league where you can pick up your groceries and two points on the same night."

New York Rangers coach **Herb Brooks,** *on the popularity of forward Ron Duguay:*

> "Even my wife likes Ron Duguay. How would you like to go home every night and see Duguay's picture on your wife's dressing table?"

Pittsburgh Penguins coach **Eddie Johnston:**

> "My team only has trouble winning in two places — Canada and the United States."

TORONTO MAPLE LEAFS COACH MIKE NYKOLUK, ON **DON CHERRY:**

"THE ONLY WAY TO BROADEN CHERRY'S MIND IS WITH A STICK OF DYNAMITE IN EACH EAR."

Edmonton Oilers coach **Glen Sather:**

> "Even a fire hydrant could score 50 goals with Wayne Gretzky at centre."

Madison Square Gardens boss **Sonny Werblin,** *downplaying the importance of the general manager and giving more credit to the coach:*

> "Anyone can shop for the groceries but it takes a real chef to prepare a meal."

King Clancy, *describing his position at Maple Leaf Gardens:*

> "Big wheel, no spin."

Al Baron, *a former governor of the Eastern Hockey League, talking about the telegram he received from his fellow-governors after undergoing surgery:*

> "It was really nice of them. They wished me a speedy recovery — by a vote of 5-4."

New York Islanders defenceman **Denis Potvin,** *talking about general manager Bill Torrey:*

> "Torrey is so shrewd, that if he had been General Custer at the Little Big Horn, not only would he have won the battle but he would have traded for the two best Indians."

Toronto Maple Leafs executive **Conn Smythe:**

> "If you can't beat 'em in the alley, you can't beat 'em on the ice."

Herb Brooks, *the coach of the U.S. gold-medal hockey team at the 1980 Lake Placid Olympics, on the made-for-TV movie of the event:*

> "My wife was hoping that Robert Redford or Paul Newman would get my role, so then she could play herself."

Vancouver Canucks general manager **Harry Neale,** after goaltender Curt Ridley injured both knees on one play:

> "What Ridley did was truly remarkable but the record is still three."

Harold Ballard, *on speculation Saskatoon might get an NHL franchise:*

> "Saskatchewan? That's where God left his snowshoes."

Fred Shero:

> "You can't really tell anything about a player until you've coached him. Let me coach a man for one year and at the end of that time I'll tell you more about him than even his wife knows."

Vancouver newspaper columnist **Jim Taylor,** *talking about the reluctance of Canucks general manager Jack Gordon to make any trades:*

> "Gordon couldn't or wouldn't make a trade if the Indians offered him Manhattan Island because it would mean giving up his best glass beads and trinkets."

Montreal Canadiens coach **Scotty Bowman,** *on winning and losing:*

> "The biggest factor that players must realize is that they can't have a crutch. You can't give them anything to blame."

Pittsburgh Penguins coach **Eddie Johnston,** *when asked who his starting goaltender would be:*

> "I'll play Roberto Romano if his equipment arrives in time from Baltimore, and if it doesn't, I'll play him anyway."

Vancouver Canucks coach **Bill Laforge:**

> "To me, Ph.D. means Pride, Hustle and Desire. If you have those qualities, you will be successful in anything."

Harold Ballard, *after NHL president John Ziegler threatened to fine him for putting advertising on the boards at Maple Leaf Gardens:*

> "If he fines me, I might have to break his neck."

Harry Neale, *following a poor performance by his team:*

> "The best thing about the game was the hot dog I had beforehand."

New York Rangers coach **Muzz Patrick,** *on his carefree approach to hockey:*

> "Why worry? There are only three things you can do — win, lose, or tie."

Roger Neilson, *on body-checking for minor hockey players:*

> "I think the whole idea for kids 10-and-under or 12-and-under is to carry the puck and skate. It's just like playing a ball hockey game. If there's body-checking in it, then it's not much of a game because you've got to be worried about that. But if it's a game where you can just free-wheel and run and pass and stickhandle, then it's a great game. I think that's what the young kids should be doing."

Boston Bruins coach **Gerry Cheevers:**

> "If I walk into a bar and there are four Bruins sitting there, I don't want them to scatter just because the coach walks in. I want to sit down and have a beer with them same as always, especially if they pick up the cheque."

NHL president **Clarence Campbell:**

> "International hockey is just a diversion. Fans know NHL hockey is the best."

Detroit Red Wings general manager **Jim Devellano,** *talking about all the fan mail for Ron Duguay:*

> "We're trying to get a special zip code just for Doogie's locker."

Buffalo Sabres coach **Jim Schoenfeld,** *after his team played a bad game:*

> "You can lead a horse to water but you can't put a bathing suit on him."

Toronto Maple Leafs coach **Floyd Smith,** *to the media following a dismal performance by his team:*

> "I have nothing to say, and I'm only going to say it once."

New York Rangers coach **Herb Brooks,** *speculating on what he might do if he were fired:*

> "On this team I've got Americans, Canadians, Venezuelans, Finns, Swedes and Czechs. I can always get a job with the United Nations."

CHAPTER 3

BASEBALL PLAYERS

"Now I look like a taco."

If you read the baseball record books, you will see such great names as Hank Aaron, Babe Ruth, Pete Rose, Ted Williams, Mickey Mantle, Reggie Jackson, Joe DiMaggio and so many others. These names are legendary and they give baseball its rich tradition.

One name you will not find in the books, however, is that of **Shawn Skinner,** and yet Shawn holds a record of some distinction — 'most innings played with a bee in your pants.'

It happened a few years ago in Wenatchee, Wash. Shawn, who was seven at the time, played several innings with a bee in his pants. Nobody knows for sure how many innings and the bee isn't telling.

"I noticed an itching early in the game," reported Shawn. "But I just thought it was a sliver or something. Then a few innings later this bee just flew right out of my pants."

His coach was impressed with Shawn's play that day, especially in light of the circumstances.

"Shawn had an outstanding game defensively," said the coach. "He had several ground balls and didn't bumble any of them."

So, just like Lou Gehrig's 2,130 consecutive games, Joe DiMaggio's 56-game hitting streak and Hank Aaron's 755 home runs, Shawn Skinner's record is one which will likely never be broken. After all, who's willing to try?

Kansas City Royals infielder **George Brett,** *on his ultimate dream:*

"To dive into the stands for a pop-up, catch the ball and at the same time take a big swig of some guy's beer."

New York Yankees slugger **Reggie Jackson:**

"I don't want to be a hero. I don't want to be a star. It just works out that way."

Philadelphia Phillies pitcher **Tug McGraw:**

"The reason the Irish are fighting each other is that they have no other worthy opponents."

Jay Johnstone *of the Los Angeles Dodgers, talking about Steve Garvey:*

"Steve is the kind of guy who, for laughs, does impersonations of Tom Landry."

Dizzy Dean, *when told his toe was fractured:*

"Fractured! The thing's broken."

Cincinnati Reds catcher **Johnny Bench:**

"I take cortisone shots for both knees. I take butazolidin, endizine and muscle relaxer. If I were a race horse I'd be disqualified."

Pittsburgh Pirates slugger **Willie Stargell,** *talking about his feeling of frustration when a knee injury forced him out of the line-up:*

"I went to the unemployment office the other day and asked them what the salary was for being frustrated. They told me frustration only pays 17 cents an hour. So you see, it doesn't even pay to be frustrated."

St. Louis Cardinals manager **Whitey Herzog,** *comparing Willie McGee to Mickey Rivers:*

"They're the same, except Willie doesn't play the horses."

Pete Rose, *on maintaining his enthusiasm after 20 years in the major leagues:*

"It doesn't take much to get me up for a baseball game. Once the national anthem plays I get chills. I even know the words to it now."

Bob Uecker, *on the lack of recognition he received during his baseball career:*

"They once had a Bob Uecker 'Day Off' for me in Philly."

Ellis Clary, *talking about his short career with the Washington Senators:*

> "My coordination was so bad I had to pull my car off to the side of the road to blow the horn."

Detroit Tigers third baseman **Aurelio Rodriguez:**

> "When I came out of Mexico, I knew only three words in English — ham and eggs. I ate ham and eggs for 10 days, breakfast, lunch and dinner. Finally, someone taught me the word 'steak.' "

Cleveland Indians third baseman **Toby Harrah:**

> "It took me 12 seasons to become an overnight sensation."

Baltimore Orioles pitcher **Dave Leonhard,** *talking about former teammate Jim Palmer:*

> "He caused me a lot of aggravation. He taught me to play golf and he introduced me to my wife."

Chicago Cubs infielder **Richie Hebner,** *bragging about his father who works in a cemetery:*

> "He's up for 'Digger of the Month.' He's eight bodies ahead of last year. He's already had a couple of hat tricks."

Former minor league baseball player **Jay Schroeder,** *on why he chose a career in professional football:*

> "I helped put Dwight Gooden in the majors and he helped put me in football."

California Angels pitcher **Ron Romanick,** *talking about the adjustment to the cold weather in Kansas City:*

> "It's pretty difficult because we've been in heat for a month."

Graig Nettles *of the New York Yankees, declining an invitation to attend a state fair:*

> "Why should I leave a circus to go to a fair?"

Los Angeles Dodgers veteran **Rick Monday,** *after the 1983 season:*

> "I'm going to play one more year. It's bad luck to retire in an odd-numbered year."

31

California Angels outfielder **Fred Lynn,** *complaining about the bad weather the club had played in for several days:*

> "If you're going to have a picnic, don't invite the Angels. We're worse than ants."

Baseball Hall of Famer **Cool Papa Bell,** *on aging:*

> "If you don't live to get old, you die young."

Bill Lee, *on Reggie Jackson:*

> "Reggie went to an all-white school in Philadelphia and has a terrible identity problem. That has forced him to be better than he might have been. We rode to the all-star game together in Kansas City in '73. He talked for 42 straight minutes. It was awful."

Pete Rose, *after a mediocre seaon:*

> "All I know is that I've won every award there is to win in this game except 'comeback player of the year,' which I'll win next year."

New York Mets centrefielder **Mookie Wilson,** *when asked by a reporter for his home telephone number:*

> "I forget. You'll have to call my wife to find out."

Pittsburgh Pirates pitcher **Jim Rooker:**

> "Manager Chuck Tanner used to have a bedcheck for me every night and my bed was always there."

New York Yankees outfielder **Oscar Gamble,** *talking about all the shuffling of team personnel because of trades and players coming up from the minors:*

> "If George Steinbrenner had given the Yankee airlines account to Braniff, they'd still be in business."

Detroit Tigers outfielder **Kirk Gibson,** *on teammate Dave Rozema:*

> "He has the kind of mind that takes an hour-and-a-half to watch '60 Minutes.' "

Boston Red Sox catcher **Carlton Fisk,** *who was known to yell at teammates when they were not giving their best:*

> "This is a business, not a tea party."

Kansas City Royals shortstop **U.L. Washington,** *on George Brett:*

> "After a while you learn from just watching George 'cause George is where it's happening. There's always something going on where he's at."

Former great **Pee Wee Reese,** *on baseball:*

> "Quick out of the clubhouse, quick out of baseball."

Rocky Bridges, *who spent 11 years in major league baseball, on his greatest ambition:*

> "I'd like to have my name in the New York Times Sunday crossword puzzle. That would be the pinnacle."

Tim McCarver, *after his retirement from baseball:*

> "The best part of being retired is showering alone."

Pittsburgh Pirates third baseman **Bill Madlock,** *on the St. Louis Cardinals outfielders:*

> "They get to everything but they don't always catch it."

Brooks Robinson, *former Baltimore Orioles great, after Graig Nettles of the New York Yankees had broken his career mark for most home runs by a third baseman:*

> "I wish someone would hit into five triple plays. I wouldn't mind losing that record too."

Jim Ksicinski, *the manager of the visiting locker room at Milwaukee's County Stadium, on the Boston Red Sox:*

> "The music is loud. Guys are running around with a hose from the shower room, spraying everybody. Guys get thrown in the ice cooler. No doubt about it, these Red Sox are the nicest guys in the league."

Montreal Expos infielder **Tim Foli,** *explaining why he likes the contact at second base on double-play takeouts:*

> "I play better when I'm bleeding."

Texas Rangers infielder **Buddy Bell,** *about fans in Kansas City:*

> "Kansas City has great, enthusiastic fans, except those who call up and threaten to kill you."

New York Yankees great **Joe DiMaggio,** *on how naive he was early in his career:*

> "I can remember a reporter asking for a quote and I didn't know what a quote was. I thought it was some kind of soft drink."

Bill Lee, *on Pete Rose:*

> "He's like a terrier dog. He's going to get you, knock you down, bite you in the jugular and let you bleed to death."

Anonymous sportswriter:

> "If Ron Darling of the Mets and Rob Deer of the Brewers ever talk on the phone, I bet they call each other by their first names."

Willie Stargell, *during his farewell day at Three Rivers Stadium:*

> "This day will remain at the top of my experiences."

Philadelphia Phillies **Al Holland** *on his relationship with fellow-reliever Tug McGraw:*

> "I talk to Tug about things in the bullpen all the time. But neither of us has an elevator that goes to the top floor, so mostly we talk from the waist down."

Bill Lee, *talking about reincarnation:*

> "I hope to come back as a grain in the field and get turned into some of the finest Dortmunder Union beer in Germany, and then have Pele drink me."

Seattle Mariners pitcher **Bill Caudill,** *discussing a game at which the crowd numbered less than 8,000:*

> "It was so quiet in there I heard a guy in the upper deck burp. Then I heard a woman in the left field stands yell: 'Pardon you.' "

Reggie Jackson, *talking about his importance to the New York Yankees:*

> "I'm the straw that stirs the drink."

Tom Seaver, *on his wife's great ability to adjust when they moved to Chicago from New York:*

> "She has already applied for a credit card from Marshall Field's."

BOB UECKER, ON HIS VALUE TO THE ST. LOUIS CARDINALS:

LITTLE FOOT · BIG FOOT

FITTING CHART

B.U.

"THE MANAGER USED TO GIVE ME ALL THE NEW SHOES TO BREAK IN SO THE OTHER PLAYERS WOULDN'T GET BLISTERS."

Steve Garvey, *after he moved from Dodger blue to Padre brown:*
"I used to look like the American flag. Now I look like a taco."

Kansas City Royals DH **Hal McRae,** *when asked what he was going to do during the baseball strike:*
"I'm going to boogaloo and barbecue."

Cleveland Indians outfielder **George Vukovich,** *shouting to the stadium crew during a home game at Municipal Stadium:*
"Don't tear the spider webs down. That's what's holding the stadium up."

Cincinnati Reds outfielder **Paul Householder:**
"I'm a household name but not a household word."

Texas Rangers outfielder **Mickey Rivers,** *as chairman of the club's kangaroo court, passing sentence on teammate Buddy Bell:*
"You threw three helmets at two dollars per helmet. Three and two is five, so you owe $5 Buddy."

Morganna Roberts, *baseball's famous 'Kissing Bandit':*
"I kiss them all on the cheek because I hate chewing tobacco. And when the cops are chasing you, you don't have time to find out if a guy is chewing bubble gum or tobacco."

California Angels second baseman **Bobby Grich:**
"I spent 15 years honing my skills, $110 at a tanning salon and $35 having my hair styled — and then I get benched on national secretaries day. There's no justice."

Pete Rose, *explaining why he got married the day before the Expos flew to Montreal for their home-opener:*
"We had to get married. That's the only way she could get on the team plane. They don't fly girlfriends, only wives."

Elliot Maddox *of the New York Mets:*
"I have an off-season vocabulary and a during-season vocabulary. I guess you could say I'm bilingual."

Willie Stargell, *on his goal entering his 20th season:*

> "I want to steal three bases this year. That would give me 20 for my career — one for each year."

Cincinnati Reds outfielder **Dave Collins,** *who was often replaced for defensive purposes in the late innings:*

> "I was out mowing my lawn the other day. I got the front done and about half the back and then I kept waiting for Sam Mejias to come out and finish it for me."

California Angels catcher **Bob Boone,** *on how he tries to relax after a game:*

> "I don't feel like reading Nietzche, I just want to watch Popeye cartoons."

Debbie Honeycutt, *wife of Seattle Mariners pitcher Rick Honeycutt, when asked to vote for the best-looking player in baseball:*

> "Are we judging from the neck up or neck down or both?"

Reggie Jackson, *trying to hype his book which included segments on the New York Yankees:*

> "When George Steinbrenner reads my book, he'll think 'The Towering Inferno' was a wiener roast."

Bill Lee, *on Carl Yastrzemski's longevity:*

> "He has lasted so long because he has a small centre of gravity. He's compact, not really vulnerable. Of course, it could be the scotch too. It numbs the pain."

Rick Monday, *on an opponent with plenty of talent but a bad attitude:*

> "He's a $40-million airport with a $30 control tower."

New York Mets pitcher **Tug McGraw:**

> "Ya gotta believe."

New York Times columnist **Red Smith,** *following the death of Yankees great Elston Howard:*

> "The Yankees lost more class on the weekend than George Steinbrenner could buy in 10 years."

Philadelphia Phillies catcher **Tim McCarver,** *after a false fire alarm in the team's hotel:*

"It was the hottest this club has been in three weeks."

Sparky Anderson, *on Pete Rose:*

"He's a complex street fighter who loves a challenge."

Former Detroit Tiger **Roger 'Doc' Cramer,** *on teammate Charlie Gehringer:*

"You wind him up on opening day and forget him."

Baltimore Orioles pitcher **Jim Palmer,** *explaining the advantage he has over young players:*

"I like to think I'm more worldly. After all, I've been to Cleveland."

Cesar Cedeno, *on why he insisted on wearing No. 28 after being traded from Houston to Cincinnati:*

"It's just that I have so much jewelry with 28 on it."

Richie Hebner *of the New York Mets, talking about a sparse crowd in Pittsburgh:*

"My father's cemetery has more life in it than this ballpark."

Yogi Berra, *explaining why he never plays a round of golf on days when his team is scheduled at night:*

"I don't like to take two showers on the same day."

Baseball veteran **Ron Fairly,** *explaining how he can be just as fast at the age of 39 as he was at the beginning of his career:*

"I had no speed to lose."

Detroit Tigers first baseman **Jason Thompson,** *after manager Sparky Anderson banned jeans on team flights:*

"There goes my wardrobe."

Steve Garvey, *after a skunk walked onto the field at Jack Murphy Stadium:*

"The longer you play this game, the more you see. I've seen streakers, cats and dogs but this was the first time I'd ever been skunk-delayed."

Pitching great **Early Wynn:**
> "When I first left home I was living on $1.10 a day, enough for 10 beers and a hamburger."

Yankees pitcher **Ron Guidry,** *when asked to compare New York with his hometown of Lafayette, La.:*
> "There's not as much night life at home as there is here. And there's not as much day life either."

Wife of a player in the World Series, to her husband:
> "Would you please stop swinging at the first pitch. You're not giving the TV people enough time to get me on camera."

Comedian **Jackie Kahane,** after Pete Rose left the Cincinnati Reds to join the Philadelphia Phillies:
> "Pete Rose left Cincinnati because of religious persecution. The Reds wouldn't recognize him as God."

Paul Simon, *in his song 'Mrs. Robinson':*
> "Where have you gone Joe DiMaggio? A nation turns its lonely eyes to you."

Joe Morgan, *in a telegram to Willie Stargell during 'Willie Stargell Day' at Three Rivers Stadium in Pittsburgh:*
> "Some people are only superstars statistically but you are a .400 hitter as a person. When I grow up, I want to be just like you."

New York Yankees third baseman **Graig Nettles,** *after he was elected team captain:*
> "What do I do, flip a coin and elect to receive?

Oakland A's pitcher **Matt Keough,** *trying to pinpoint the reason for a team slump:*
> "Our home uniforms are too tight."

Los Angeles Dodgers catcher **Roy Campanella:**
> "You gotta be a man to play baseball for a living but you gotta have a lot of little boy in you too."

Paul Householder, *who became engaged on New Year's Eve:*
> "With the kind of year I had, I'm ready to try anything."

Reggie Jackson, *when asked how many seasons it would take his new team, the California Angels, to get to the World Series:*

"It will only take three — spring, summer and fall."

Bill Lee:

"According to Margaret Mead, Buckminster Fuller and a lot of other people, the reason the Roman Empire became extinct was that it had too many specialists. You can see the same thing happening to baseball."

New York Mets pitcher **Rick Ownbey,** *as he entered the clubhouse for the first time after being called up from the minors:*

"Where's the water fountain?"

Jan Kern, *wife of Texas Rangers pitcher Jim Kern, after her husband shaved off a full set of whiskers:*

"Now I remember why I liked the beard."

Bob Uecker, *talking about success:*

"Real achievement is making the big leagues without any talent, like me."

U.L. Washington, *trying to explain that 'U.L.' does not stand for anything:*

"I don't know why but people don't believe that I have only initials. Someone even asked me if the U.L. stands for 'Unleaded.' Can you imagine that?"

Atlanta Braves pitcher **John Montefusco,** *shortly after joining the club from the San Francisco Giants:*

"I'm really happy to be here. I feel like I just got out of jail."

George Brett, *after the team bus broke down and he hitchhiked back to the hotel:*

"I was afraid we'd get back after 9 and I'd miss 'Dallas' on TV."

Jennie Parrish, *wife of slugger Larry Parrish, after her husband began wearing glasses:*

"Things are much better now. Larry can read the menu on the wall at McDonald's while we're standing in line."

Pitcher **Bill Caudill,** *who was a member of the New York Yankees for 22 minutes before being sent to Seattle:*

> "When I retire, I'm going to ask George Steinbrenner to send me a uniform with one pinstripe on it."

Johnny Bench, *trying to explain his retirement:*

> "A catcher squats 200 times every game. If he plays 120 games a year, that's 24,000 squats. I played 13 years, or 312,000 squats. Let somebody do 312,000 squats and then come back to me and ask why I'm retiring."

Brad Lesley, *a 6'6", 230-pound relief pitcher for the Cincinnati Reds, talking about other sports he played in high school:*

> "I was a linebacker in football and a fouler in basketball."

San Francisco Giants pitcher **Dave LaPoint,** *about a game at which the crowd was only 1,632:*

> "It was the first game in major league history where everyone in the stands got a foul ball."

Bill Lee:

> "Baseball should be played on natural grass. It's nice and soft and it grows and you don't get hurt."

Pete Rose:

> "Baseball is my whole life. It's what I know best."

CHAPTER 4

PITCHERS

"Throw peas at their knees."

Minor league pitcher **Mark Lee** had decided to retire at the end of the season. He planned to make the official announcement right after the last game. In that last game, Lee took the field for the ninth inning. He struck out the first batter and then struck out the second. Then, curiously, Lee waved his manager to the mound, handed him the ball and told him of his decision to retire. While the manager stood speechless, Lee casually strolled through the dugout to the clubhouse, his career over.

Following the game, Lee faced reporters and teammates to explain his unusual action.

"I didn't want to take a chance against another hitter," he confessed, "because I always wanted to strike out the last man I ever faced in pro ball."

Los Angeles Dodgers outfielder **Rick Monday,** *talking about the knuckleball of Atlanta's Phil Niekro:*

"It actually giggles at you as it goes by."

Blanche Perry, *wife of notorious spitball pitcher Gaylord Perry, talking about her difficulty in playing catch with her husband during the off-season:*

"The ball is always wet and hard to grip."

Kansas City Royals relief pitcher **Dan Quisenberry,** *on what it's like to pitch in the Minneapolis Metrodome:*

"There's no safe lead in this yard. There's no fail-safe zone. It's condition red all the time."

New York Mets pitcher **Tom Seaver,** *after throwing a one-hitter:*

"No, I'm not upset at missing the no-hitter. I once missed a hole-in-one by only three strokes."

Jim Bunning, *on why he always tries to keep the ball low:*

"Have you ever seen a 450-foot ground ball?"

Reggie Jackson, *on New York Yankees pitcher Ron Guidry:*

"His stats speak for themselves. You don't buy 'em at the supermarket."

New York Yankees pitcher **Tommy John,** *talking about his elbow surgery:*

"When they operated on my arm, I asked them to put in a Koufax fastball. They did but it was a Mrs. Koufax fastball."

Oakland A's pitcher **Steve McCatty:**

"I enjoy being a reliever because I like getting six outs for the same money as getting 27."

Slugger **Richie Ashburn,** *on Dodgers pitcher Don Drysdale:*

"I had a real good look at the first pitch I ever saw from Drysdale. If I hadn't ducked, it would have hit me right between the eyes."

Mike Krukow, *after he pitched for three different teams in three seasons:*

"People ask me where I live and I tell them 'in escrow.' "

Original New York Mets pitcher **Roger Craig,** *after he threw out the ceremonial first ball at the club's 25th anniversary celebration.*

"They should have had the bases loaded, because every time I pitched for them that's what happened."

Kansas City Royals pitcher **Rich Gale,** *after a reporter asked him: 'What's up?':*

"Oh, my fastball, my slider and my ERA."

Baltimore Orioles pitcher **Jim Palmer,** *when he learned Earl Weaver would step down as manager after 1982:*

"I'll probably have my best year in '83."

Retired fireballer **Bob Feller,** *when asked how fast he could still throw:*

> "I've joined the energy crisis. I'm going by the guidelines, throwing it 55 m.p.h."

Houston Astros pitcher **Joe Niekro,** *talking about rookie catcher George Bjorkman:*

> "I only had one problem with George. I couldn't see his signs the first few innings. He's not tanned enough and I can't distinguish his hand from our white uniforms. I'm going to get him some Coppertone."

Montreal Expos pitcher **Bill Lee,** *after giving up a home run to Bob Horner of Atlanta:*

> "I should have walked him. He walked anyway. That ball would have cleared the Grand Canyon."

Richie Ashburn, *on hitting against Bob Gibson:*

> "When he was on the mound, I always felt like I was standing at the plate dressed as the Grand Dragon of the Ku Klux Klan."

Seattle Mariners pitcher **Gaylord Perry,** *downplaying his defensive inabilities:*

> "If I had wanted to catch ground balls, I would have been a shortstop."

Dan Quisenberry, *on the control problems plaguing Royals teammate Renie Martin:*

> "Some people throw to spots, some people throw to zones. Renie throws to continents."

Philadelphia Phillies pitcher **Tug McGraw,** *talking about the good days and bad days experienced by relievers:*

> "Some days you tame the tiger and some days the tiger has you for lunch."

Toronto Blue Jays manager **Bobby Cox,** *after a pitcher argued he should stay in the game by pointing out that he had struck out the next batter the last time he faced him:*

> "Yes, I remember. It was earlier this inning."

Texas Rangers pitching coach **Jackie Brown,** *explaining why he had never been ejected during his days as a pitcher:*

"I never had to argue balls and strikes, because if I threw one over the plate someone always smacked the daylights out of it. There was never any question."

Johnny Bench, *on Jim Kaat, one of the quickest-working pitchers in baseball:*

"Jim has been in the game 24 years but he has only been on the mound an elapsed time of five hours."

Houston Astros third baseman **Enos Cabell,** *on the trouble with playing behind pitcher Nolan Ryan:*

"He throws so many pitches that you have to walk around out there to keep yourself in the game."

Milwaukee Brewers reliever **Rollie Fingers,** *after losing four of five games he entered with the score tied:*

"The next tie game I come into, I'm going to stand there until it rains. I'm not going to throw the ball. I'm just going to wait for it to rain."

Chicago White Sox advance scout **Loren Babe,** *on how to pitch to the Milwaukee Brewers:*

"It's very simple. Keep it low and outside and high and inside and make sure it's low and outside and high and inside."

Satchell Paige, *on his philosophy of pitching:*

"Throw peas at their knees."

San Francisco Giants pitcher **Bill Laskey,** *after he tossed a 7-0 shutout in his first major league start:*

"This is my first dream-come-true in the big leagues and until I read about it in the newspapers, I'm not going to believe it happened."

Baltimore Orioles pitcher **Mike Flanagan,** *after he missed an assignment, breaking a streak of 157 consecutive starts:*

"It's just an oil change and a 3,000-inning check-up."

Sal Maglie, *on why he often threw two brushback pitches at certain batters:*

> "The second one was to make sure he understood the first one."

Rick Monday, *explaining why he asked the umpire to check the ball after one of Don Sutton's pitches:*

> "The ball sunk about three feet, so it either ran into a swarm of medflies between the mound and home plate, or it went through a car wash."

Bill Lee:

> "I never again want to be taken out of the starting rotation and I want Fred Kendall to catch me every time because he needs a purpose in life."

Chicago Cubs pitcher **Lynn McGlothen,** *on speculation that most of the team might be traded:*

> "Who'd want any of us?"

Sportswriter **Jim Proudfoot,** *after the Toronto Blue Jays signed Korean pitcher Don Wong Choi:*

> "The Jays will be glad to have him as long as he doesn't give up too many 'woks.' "

Dan Quisenberry, *explaining how he felt when he broke the record with his 39th save of the season:*

> "Tonight I really got excited. I really felt good. It was a real thrill. I took my hat off and everything."

Los Angeles Dodgers pitcher **Jerry Reuss,** *talking about the advantages of experience:*

> "If you think it's an advantage, it is. If the other team thinks it is, it's a bigger advantage. Actually, it means nothing."

Former Los Angeles Dodgers catcher **Johnny Roseboro,** *when asked what was the most important quality a catcher had to have:*

> "The ability to babysit the pitchers."

Toronto Blue Jays relief pitcher **Bill Caudill,** *trying to explain a bad day on the mound:*

> "Even Betty Crocker burns a cake now and then."

Chicago White Sox outfielder **Ron Kittle,** *after his team was no-hit by Detroit's Jack Morris:*

> "I'm part of history but I'm on the wrong end. I would have preferred to watch him bowl a 300 game."

Satchell Paige:

> "Don't look back, something may be gaining on you."

Toronto Blue Jays pitcher **Jim Gott,** *after giving up a game-winning home run to Dave Kingman of Oakland:*

> "I was trying to pitch Dave up and in and he hit it up and in — up to row 45 in Section 24."

Detroit Tigers manager **Sparky Anderson,** *on pitchers:*

> "Nolan Ryan has a good fastball, Joe Niekro has a good knuckleball, some guys have good screwballs and Gaylord Perry has a good something."

Jim Kaat, *on his retirement:*

> "I have no complaints. I had a 25-year vacation."

Oakland A's pitcher **Steve McCatty,** *after the fans gave the club a season-ending standing ovation despite the fact it finished more than 20 games out of first place:*

> "Can you imagine this in New York? They'd call us back all right — for an execution."

Dan Quisenberry:

> "The most exciting thing about my season so far is forming the only Q-initialled battery in baseball, me and Jamie Quirk."

Minnesota Twins pitcher **Pete Redfern,** *talking about the small crowds at the Metrodome:*

> "It's sick. Talk about 'SRO.' At the dome it's Sitting Room Only."

Los Angeles Dodgers catcher **Mike Scioscia,** *on rookie pitcher Fernando Valenzuela:*

> "He only knows three words in English — food, beer and light beer."

Doug Rader, *when asked to name the five best pitchers he ever faced:*

> "Bob Gibson in 1968, Bob Gibson in 1969, Bob Gibson in 1970, Bob Gibson in 1971 and Bob Gibson in 1972."

Johnny Bench, *after pitcher Paul Moskau was traded:*

> "I'll miss Paul. He was our fourth in bridge and he owes me money."

Satchell Paige, *when asked why he took so long walking from the bullpen to the mound:*

> "Do you expect me to rush into that?"

St. Louis Cardinals slugger **Stan Musial,** *on Clem Labine:*

> "Let me tell you this, Clem Labine was a mighty tough pitcher, one of the toughest I ever faced. I don't think my lifetime batting average against him was higher than .295."

Dan Quisenberry, *when told that his records this year were better than he had last year:*

> "How did you know? I'm into classical this year instead of pop."

New York Yankees pitcher **Rudy May,** *on how to pitch to Kansas City's George Brett:*

> "The only thing to do is pitch him way inside, so you force him to pull the ball. That way, the line drive won't hit you."

Oakland A's pitcher **Steve McCatty,** *giving advice to opposing pitchers on how to deal with base-stealer Rickey Henderson when he gets on first base:*

> "Wind up real slow and hope there's a close play at third."

Oakland A's pitcher **Brian Kingman,** *amid rumors he was about to be traded:*

> "I'm the only player on the team with a perforated page in the media guide. It makes it easier to take out when I'm traded."

Sportscaster **Ralph Kiner,** *describing the way Phil Niekro throws a knuckleball:*

> "It's like watching Mario Andretti park a car."

Minnesota Twins scout **Ellis Clary,** *on a new pitching prospect:*

"I'd rather have his future than my past."

Former major league pitcher **Dave McNally,** *who lives in Billings, Mont., talking about San Francisco 49ers quarterback Joe Montana:*

"Joe is kinda like our weather. No matter what the date, he's cool."

Bill Lee:

"My hero was Jim Kaat. He was around so long they had to put his career on microfilm."

Los Angeles Dodgers pitcher **Orel Hershiser,** *when asked if being deeply religious hurt his aggressiveness:*

"Being a Christian doesn't mean you have to be a wimp."

Milwaukee Brewers pitcher **Don Sutton,** *after serving up a home run:*

"I wanted him to hit the ball right at somebody. Unfortunately, the guy he hit the ball at paid $3.50 for his seat."

Gaylord Perry, *when asked what his goals were after he reached 300 career wins:*

"I'd like to play some other position and I'd like to steal a base."

Anonymous scout, about a pitching prospect:

"He ain't got much stuff but he throws hard enough to put a strawberry through the side of a submarine."

Texas Rangers pitcher **Mike Smithson,** *after he had six of his first 10 big league starts marred by rain:*

"I could get rained out in the Astrodome."

Dan Quisenberry, *while accepting the top reliever award:*

"I want to thank all of our pitchers who couldn't go nine innings and manager Dick Howser who wouldn't let them."

Pittsburgh Pirates pitcher **John Candelaria,** *after hitting his first home run in more than 500 at-bats:*

> "I had a good idea it was a homer. I've thrown so many to other hitters I recognized the sound."

St. Louis Cardinals relief pitcher **Bruce Sutter,** *when a reporter suggested he had lost weight:*

> "You would too if you'd backed up third base as often as I have this year."

Oakland A's pitcher **Jay Howell,** *explaining his success:*

> "I throw the ball as hard as I can and hope they hit it to Alfredo Griffin."

Pittsburgh Pirates relief pitcher **Kent Tekulve,** *on his 2-9 record:*

> "I feel like I have a cobra wrapped around my neck.

St. Louis Cardinals manager **Whitey Herzog,** *after one of his pitchers gave up 16 hits and 10 runs in just five innings:*

> "He got hit so hard I had to get all the married men off the infield."

Cleveland Indians pitcher **Jamie Easterly,** *talking about a pitch he threw for a three-run home run:*

> "I tried to throw him a sinker and it sunk about 390 feet away."

Toronto Blue Jays manager **Bobby Cox,** *to a pitcher who had just given up a grand slam home run:*

> "Don't worry about it. It was a great pitch for the first 60 feet."

Satchell Paige, *on pitching:*

> "Throw it there when they're lookin' here, and throw it here when they're lookin' there."

Don Drysdale, *on his philosophy of pitching:*

> "My challenge to the hitter is: 'You take one half of the plate and I'll take the other half. I'm just not telling you which half is mine.' "

Former major league pitching coach **Art Fowler,** *who had a lengthy career despite his lack of respect for training rules and curfews:*

> "I pitched in more than 1,000 games over 20 years and was still pitching when I was 48. I couldn't have done better if I'd lived in an iron lung and gone to church twice every Sunday."

Dan Quisenberry:

> "I don't really have good stuff, just some controlled slop."

Bob Feller, *when asked if he threw harder in his prime than New York Yankees reliever Rich Gossage:*

> "I would hope so."

Texas Rangers pitcher **Charlie Hough:**

> "They say most good managers were mediocre players. I should be a heckuva manager."

Jim Kaat, *who pitched in the majors more than 20 years:*

> "I'll never be considered one of the all-time greats, maybe not even one of the all-time goods. But I'm one of the all-time survivors."

Oakland A's pitcher **Matt Keough,** *after snapping a personal 18-game losing streak:*

> "I learned a lot but I don't want to learn it again."

Bill Lee, *on the chances of his returning to the Montreal Expos' starting rotation:*

> "It would be easier to break into Fort Knox. One of our starters would have to drop dead and they're all younger than I am."

San Francisco Giants pitcher **Greg Minton,** *when asked his goals for the upcoming season:*

> "This year, I'd like to steal a team plane."

Promising right-hander **Rick Ownbey,** *talking about some of his problems at spring training:*

> "The Cards wanted me to throw the ball over the plate but I can't pitch that way."

Gaylord Perry, *after he retired from baseball:*

> "I'm not going to say if I ever threw a spitball. The only thing I'll say is it's going to be a little drier around the American League."

California Angels pitcher **Frank Tanana:**

> "If my teammates give me one run, I should win the game."

Don Sutton, *when asked if he 'doctors' the ball with hidden sandpaper:*

> "Of course not. Sandpaper gets wet and crumbles."

Dan Quisenberry, *trying to describe his style:*

> "I'm not a Mercedes but a Volkswagen. I don't go fast but you can get a lot of mileage out of me."

Los Angeles Dodgers manager **Tommy Lasorda,** *describing Hall of Famer Don Drysdale:*

> "He pitched like my wife shops — all day."

Detroit Tigers manager **Sparky Anderson,** *on Gaylord Perry's spitball:*

> "I can't knock it. He's got more wins than I had hits — by about 200."

Hall of Fame pitcher **Early Wynn:**

> "The first thing I do when I wake up in the morning is breathe on a mirror and hope it fogs up."

Cleveland Indians pitcher **Jamie Easterly,** *reporting a rash on his arm to his manager:*

> "The doctor says I can't run for the rest of the season and I can only drink Chivas Regal."

Dan Quisenberry, *talking about a ball hit hard right back up the middle:*

> "That ball played pinball wizard on my legs, lit up all the bonus lights and even got a free game."

Minnesota Twins **Bobby Castillo,** *on pitching in the Metrodome:*

> "A pitchers need two things here — a calculator to figure out his ERA and a good sense of humor."

Phil Niekro, *when asked how he stays in shape:*

"By polka dancing."

Jim Kaat:

"The way I see it, there's the Hall of Fame and the Hall of Achievement and there's also the Hall of Enjoyment. I hope to be enshrined in the Hall of Enjoyment."

Sportscaster **Al Michaels,** *commenting on the new style used by Oakland A's pitcher Steve McCatty:*

"He's got a new pitch he calls 'the nudist.' It's got absolutely nothing on it."

Kansas City Royals pitcher **Rich Gale,** *after a bad outing:*

"I was super in the first inning. In the second I eroded in parts and in the third I completely disappeared."

Boston Red Sox pitcher **Bob Stanley,** *on what he learned from Gaylord Perry's suspension for throwing a spitball:*

"I'm not going to throw it any more, if I ever did, and I can't remember."

New York Mets pitcher **Randy Myers,** *after he discovered the zipper on his uniform pants was broken:*

"I was afraid they'd call me on the infield fly rule."

CHAPTER 5

HITTERS AND FIELDERS

"He could hit buckshot with a barbed wire."

Babe Ruth and **Jimmie Reese** were teammates with the New York Yankees in the early 1930s. In fact, for a while during Reese's rookie year in 1930, the two were roommates.

At the time, Ruth was the popular veteran, the slugger who once belted 60 home runs in a single season and the man who was quickly carving out his own legend in the game. Reese was a rookie, a light-hitting second baseman and a man who wasn't even a legend in his own mind.

"I remember one incident in my rookie year," Reese recalls. "We trailed Cleveland 6-3 in the ninth inning. I got up there with the bases loaded. Bob Shawkey was our manager with the Yankees and he told me to run like crazy if I hit the ball on the ground. The Babe was up next and we didn't want any double plays to end the game. I hit a grand slam off Wes Ferrell to win it 7-6. When I rounded the bases, the Babe was waiting for me at home plate. He slammed me on the back and said: 'Nice hitting, kid. Now you're only 59 behind.' "

George Brett, *during a hot hitting streak:*

"The only bad thing about my swing right now is that I can't stand back and watch it."

Mickey Mantle, *explaining why manager Billy Martin did not hire him as a New York Yankees batting instructor:*

"Billy told me: 'If we want to teach someone how to strike out, we'll call you.' "

Sportscaster **Joe Garagiola:**

"Most pitchers should have 'for display purposes only' written on their bats."

Yogi Berra, *on hitting:*

> "You can't think and hit at the same time."

Johnny Bench, *on Pete Rose:*

> "He's the most statistics-conscious player I've ever seen —
> and I wish we had eight more just like him."

Ruppert Jones, *on the best way to play the outfield in wind-
swept Candlestick Park:*

> "Pray no one hits the ball to you."

Chicago White Sox slugger **Ron Kittle,** *after he was named
American League 'rookie-of-the-year':*

> "I'm thrilled, it's exciting and I'm honored. My mom told
> me to say that last one."

Sportswriter **Joe Falls:**

> "Only two players in my life I never went out to go to the
> bathroom when they were coming up — Ted Williams and
> Mickey Mantle."

Slugger **Richie Ashburn,** *on how he cured a batting slump:*

> "I took my bats to bed. I wanted to get to know them better.
> I know it sounds a little weird but in a slump a player will do
> anything."

Montreal Expos catcher **Gary Carter,** *on the art of blocking home
plate:*

> "You only block the plate if the play is going to be close.
> Some guys want to play football out there. Not me."

New York Mets third baseman **Hubie Brooks,** *talking about a
game in which he made three errors in one inning:*

> "I don't think about it much but I do have the date written in
> my glove."

Texas Rangers manager **Doug Rader,** *on outfielder Mickey
Rivers:*

> "Mickey Rivers could lift weights all day every day and his
> throws wouldn't bruise a baby's lips."

Atlanta Braves utility man **Mike Lum,** *after a brilliant catch against the New York Mets:*

"Just imagine what I'd do if I practised."

Toby Harrah *of the Cleveland Indians:*

"Statistics are like a girl in a bikini. It shows a lot but it doesn't show everything."

Catfish Hunter, *on former teammate Reggie Jackson:*

"Reggie would give you the shirt off his back if you needed it. Of course, he'd call a press conference to announce it."

Pete Rose, *right after his Philadelphia Phillies won the 1980 World Series:*

"We open 1981 against Cincinnati. That means Tom Seaver will be pitching and I'll go 0-for-4."

Graig Nettles, *after the New York Yankees had run themselves into a triple play:*

"What we need is a second base coach."

Speedy centre fielder **Amos Otis,** *talking about slower teammates in left and right:*

"I've had Lou Piniella in left and Ed Kirkpatrick in right. I'd start the season weighing 170 and end it at 155."

Joe DiMaggio, *on being voted baseball's greatest living player:*

"At my age, I'm happy to be named the greatest living anything."

New York Mets catcher **John Stearns,** *on slugger Dave Kingman:*

"He has got the personality of a tree trunk."

New York Mets infielder **Ray Knight,** *describing the infield at San Francisco's Candlestick Park:*

"It's like playing basketball on a cobblestone street."

Baltimore Orioles catcher **Rick Dempsey,** *talking to reporters at training camp after he had been named World Series MVP the previous fall:*

"Are you guys still writing good things about me, or are you back to telling the truth."

Boston Red Sox infielder **Jerry Remy,** *after detecting some water dripping from the roof of the Minneapolis Metrodome:*
> "Can a game be leaked out?"

Ty Cobb:
> "When we were boys in Georgia, we used to play in a cow pasture. One day I slid headfirst into what I thought was second base."

Kansas City Royals relief pitcher **Dan Quisenberry:**
> "Reggie Jackson once hit a home run off me in Kansas City and it's still on its way to St. Louis."

Montreal Expos outfielder **Warren Cromartie,** *talking about two grand slams hit by teammate Al Oliver:*
> "Heck, that must be seven or eight RBIs right there."

Pitcher **Doc Medich,** *on the base-stealing of Rickey Henderson:*
> "He's like a little kid in a train station — you turn your back on him and he's gone."

An unidentified fan in St. Louis who poured a beer over Pete Rose as he tried to catch a foul ball near the stands:
> "Hey, Pete, this Bud's for you." (The fan was ejected)

New York Mets pitcher **Tug McGraw,** *when asked how to stop Hank Aaron:*
> "Don't throw the ball."

New York Yankees infielder **Mike Pagliarulo:**
> "I've been superstitious all my career but no longer. I'm even giving up the red ribbon I wear on my athletic supporter. It's an old Italian custom to keep the evil spirits away."

Rogers Hornsby, *on why he liked baseball better than golf:*
> "When I hit a ball I want someone else to go chase it."

Los Angeles Dodgers **Bill Russell,** *on the hardest part of switching from shortstop to the outfield at the age of 35:*
> "At my age, just running out to position."

Gorman Thomas *of the Milwaukee Brewers, talking about his lack of recognition:*

"Even my fan mail arrives addressed to Thomas Gorman."

San Francisco Giants catcher **Bob Brenly,** *reflecting back on a 100-loss season:*

"Last year we considered it a rally if a batter got a 3-0 count."

Kurt Bevacqua *of the San Diego Padres:*

"I'd rather be called a role player than a utility man. I hate the word 'utility.' It sounds like I work for the electric company."

Steve Kemp *of the New York Yankees, talking about the power of teammate Dave Winfield:*

"I've never seen a man who can hit the ball so hard so many times. If I were sitting out in the bleachers, I'd go get a hot dog when he was at bat. I wouldn't want to get killed."

Rusty Staub, *talking about the Jiminy Cricket decal on the rear of his batting helmet:*

"Yes, there's a reason for it, and no, I'm not going to get into it."

Chicago White Sox pitcher **Ed Farmer,** *talking about Reggie Jackson:*

"Very few players come along in a lifetime who look as good striking out as they do hitting home runs. Reggie is never cheated at the plate and he never cheats the fans."

Pete Rose, *talking about his strategy when he nears another record:*

"Any time I come to bat with a chance to reach a plateau or record, I never hit the ball in the air. I'm afraid I'll hit a home run and never get the ball back for my collection."

Dave Parker *of the Pittsburgh Pirates, just before the opening game of the season:*

"It's time to go to work, the bell's done rung."

59

New York Yankees third baseman **Graig Nettles,** *talking about the infield grass at Tiger Stadium in Detroit:*

> "They can't have a father-son game here because the kids would get lost."

Slugger **Don Baylor,** *on playing in the Seattle Kingdome:*

> "In this park, when you walk to the plate you're in scoring position."

Detroit Tigers catcher **Lance Parrish,** *after he was hit in the head with a pitch:*

> "I was thinking about which way I'd duck if it happened, when it happened."

Oakland's **Dan Meyer,** *who went 0-for-37 while filling in for Carney Lansford:*

> "It's all Carney's fault. If he hadn't got hurt, I never would have been out there."

San Francisco sportswriter **Art Spander,** *on the winds at Candlestick Park:*

> "Where else does a shortstop spend more time chasing his cap than pop flies?"

Ron Kittle, *on one of the reasons for his success:*

> "My father always told me if you worked hard and ate your vegetables your dreams would come true."

Hank Aaron:

> "A smart hitter can set up a pitcher his first or second at-bat by purposely letting himself look foolish against a certain pitch. Then, in the late innings with runners on, the pitcher might try that same pitch again and you can hit it for extra bases."

Slugger **Rico Carty,** *when asked how he stays in shape:*

> "All I do is rub myself down with baby oil before each game."

Philadelphia Phillies outfielder **Jerry Martin,** *after breaking out of an extended slump:*

> "I hadn't hit the ball hard since Moby Dick was a minnow."

REGGIE JACKSON, DURING A BATTING SLUMP: "I'M SO BAD NOW I COULDN'T HIT A BEACHBALL."

Steve Garvey, *describing the feeling he gets when he plays at Busch Stadium in St. Louis and then goes to Wrigley Field in Chicago:*

"It's like going from a par-five to a par-three."

Reggie Jackson, *on his defensive play:*

"The only way I'm going to get a Gold Glove is with a can of spray paint."

Anonymous catcher:

"Batters aren't embarrassed after stumbling for a change-up. They're sick."

Pete Rose:

"Line drives don't take bad hops."

Catcher **Yogi Berra,** *after a hitter made the sign of the cross on home plate:*

"Let's just let Him watch today's game, okay?"

Minnesota's **Randy Bush,** *after teammate Tom Brunansky's .073 batting average was posted on the stadium scoreboard:*

"Hey, Tom, some of the lights are out on your average."

Kansas City Royals pitcher **Paul Splittorff,** *about a George Brett home run:*

"Anything that travels that far in the air ought to have a stewardess on it."

Jim Essian *of the Seattle Mariners, after hitting his first big league home run:*

"I wanted to go into my home run trot but then I realized I didn't have one."

Reggie Jackson:

"When you play this game 10 years, go to bat 7,000 times and get 2,000 hits, you know what that means? It means you've gone 0-for-5,000."

Ron Kittle, *after he failed to hit a homer during the entire month of May:*

> "I guess the only months I ever went without a home run were last November and December. If I liked failing so much, I'd have stayed in fifth-grade math."

Pete Rose:

> "I've got at least 70 hits off Phil Niekro and over 100 off Joe Niekro. Why couldn't Mrs. Niekro have had triplets?"

Houston Astros infielder **Enos Cabell,** *in the midst of a long batting slump:*

> "Nobody's nice to me any more. They keep throwing me curves and they know I can't hit them."

Dan Quisenberry, *on the Milwaukee Brewers:*

> "There aren't any quiche-eaters in that order."

Oakland A's base-stealer **Rickey Henderson,** *on his early success under manager Billy Martin:*

> "The aggressiveness I have is the aggressiveness Billy has. Between his style and my speed, we can make things happen."

San Diego Padres outfielder **Ruppert Jones,** *after he had struck out for the eighth at-bat in a row:*

> "If you go to bat 600 times in a season and you get 200 hits, it doesn't matter how you get the 400 outs."

San Francisco Giants manager **Dave Bristol,** *to his team during a hitting slump:*

> "There will be two buses leaving the hotel for the park tomorrow. The two o'clock bus will be for those of you who need a little extra batting practice. The empty bus will leave at five."

Keith Moreland *of the Philadelphia Phillies, after hitting his first career grand slam home run:*

> "I didn't even know it was a grand slam until I rounded third and saw everybody standing at home plate."

Mickey Mantle, *talking about the 565-foot home run he hit in Washington:*

> "The funniest thing about it was that Billy Martin tagged up at third base. I got all the way around to third and he's still there tagging up and the ball went over the scoreboard in left-centre."

Lenny Randle *of Seattle, after hitting a grand slam home run to give the Mariners a win over Minnesota:*

> "I'm in a coma. I almost forgot to run. That's probably my first grand slam ever and also my quota."

John Lowenstein *of the Baltimore Orioles, on what he does to keep busy during games in which he is the designated hitter:*

> "I flush the toilets between innings to keep my wrists strong."

Major league batting coach **Charley Lau:**

> "There are two theories on hitting the knuckleball. Unfortunately, neither of them works."

Yogi Berra, *on son Dale's lack of power:*

> "Sure he's hit three home runs so far this year but he's only hit them one at a time."

Pete Rose, *to the home plate umpire during a game in the snow in Montreal:*

> "This is the first time I've ever played with snow falling. If I get a hit, can I have the ball for my trophy case?"

Reggie Jackson, *near the end of his career:*

> "I'm still Reggie but not as often."

San Diego Padres pitcher **Sid Monge,** *after he was hit in the back of the head by a line drive off the bat of Montreal's Andre Dawson:*

> "I threw him a change-up. I threw it at 80 miles per hour and it came back at me at 150."

Harley Dunan, *the secretary of revenue in Kansas, explaining why he waived the vision test when George Brett applied for his drivers licence renewal:*

> "If he can hit .350, we figure he can see."

Toronto Blue Jays catcher **Buck Martinez,** *talking about his dismal season at the plate:*

"There were times this year when people looked at the scoreboard and thought my batting average was the temperature."

Pete Rose:

"I'm just like everybody else. I have two arms, two legs and 4,000 hits."

Pittsburgh Pirates outfielder **Steve Kemp,** *on a season-long batting slump:*

"It's not easy to hit .215. You have to be going terrible and have bad luck too."

Philadelphia Phillies outfielder **Bake McBride,** *talking about a streak during which he hit .609:*

"I've never had a streak like this, not even in stickball."

Hank Aaron:

"Hitting is mostly thinking."

Joe Simpson *of the Kansas City Royals, after he broke an 0-for-22 slump with a triple and was breathless at third base:*

"I'm used to making right turns at first base — those left-hand turns really got to me."

Bob Uecker, *explaining what manager Gene Mauch would tell him when he was pinch-hitting:*

"He'd tell me to grab a bat and stop this rally. Or he'd send me up there without a bat and tell me to try for a walk."

Kansas City Royals manager **Jim Frey,** *on George Brett:*

"He could hit buckshot with a barbed wire."

Boston Red Sox second baseman **Jerry Remy,** *after he hit his first home run in six years:*

"I think I may have put the pressure on myself. Now the fans will expect me to do this every six years."

Pete Rose:

"The perfect all-star game is one in which everybody has fun, nobody gets hurt and the National League wins."

San Diego Padres outfielder **Tony Gwynn,** *on his lack of power:*

"My goal this year is to hit 30 home runs, counting batting practice. I'm already up to 26, five of 'em in real games."

Kansas City's **Jerry Grote,** *who hit a grand slam home run and drove in seven runs during one game at the age of 38:*

"The older the violin, the sweeter the music."

CHAPTER 6

MANAGERS

"If he doesn't mind me, I'll tell his mother."

It was mid-season, 1981, and the Los Angeles Dodgers had just lost their seventh game in a row. All was quiet in the clubhouse as the players sat with their heads down. Manager **Tommy Lasorda** knew he had to do something to re-establish the players' belief in themselves. He strolled to the middle of the room, paused until he had everyone's attention, and then spoke.

"Get your heads up, men," he began. "You have nothing to be ashamed of. You are all great players and together you make a great team. Don't worry about a few losses, even the great teams in the game have dropped a few. As a matter of fact, the best team in baseball history, the 1927 New York Yankees, once lost nine games in a row."

The speech had impact. The Dodgers won the next night, and the next and the night after that. They rolled off nine straight wins. Eventually, they captured the National League title and the World Series.

Long after that season was history, Lasorda was reminded of his team's amazing turnaround and his speech which had been so critical in achieving it.

"I haven't the faintest idea if the '27 Yankees lost nine in a row," he confessed. "But it sure sounded good at the time, and it worked."

Baltimore Orioles manager **Earl Weaver,** *explaining why he was tossed out of so many ball games for arguing with umpires:*
"To calm my players down."

Dick Williams, *on how he managed the San Diego Padres into pennant contention:*
"I tell a guy to hit to right. He singles to left and we win."

Mrs. Joe Cronin, *to her husband every time he left the house to manage the Boston Red Sox against the Yankees:*

"Don't forget to walk Joe DiMaggio."

Chicago Cubs manager **Leo Durocher:**

"You don't save a pitcher for tomorrow. Tomorrow it may rain."

Yankees manager **Bob Lemon:**

"I drink after wins, I drink after losses, I drink after rainouts."

Tommy Lasorda:

"Your average training room today looks like the Mayo Clinic. When I was a player, our training room consisted of one trainer and one bottle of alcohol. And by the seventh inning, the trainer had usually drunk half the bottle."

Earl Weaver, *on the ailments of his star pitcher Jim Palmer:*

"The Chinese tell time by the 'Year of the Dragon' and the 'Year of the Horse.' I tell time by Palmer — the 'Year of the Shoulder,' the 'Year of the Elbow,' the 'Year of the Ulna Nerve.' "

Casey Stengel:

"Good pitchin' will always beat good hittin' and vice-versa."

Philadelphia Phillies manager **Danny Ozark,** *after a bad loss:*

"We were as flat tonight as people used to think the earth was."

Lou Brock *of St. Louis, to Tommy Lasorda:*

"I saw Johnny Carson on your show the other night."

Baseball manager, about a player who had a sensational season:

"He led the league in everything but hotel accommodations."

Billy Martin:

"First you're a man, then you're a manager."

Texas Rangers manager **Doug Rader,** *on the advantage of working in the major leagues:*

> "When a player does well, you don't have to worry about his being called up."

Earl Weaver, *after one of his players complained he wasn't given a fair chance:*

> "I gave him more chances than my first wife."

Chicago White Sox manager **Tony LaRussa,** *on why he is able to get along so well with his players:*

> "I like rock music and I understand hair dryers."

Yogi Berra, *while watching a Steve McQueen movie:*

> "They must have made this one while he was still alive."

Sparky Anderson's *daughter, when he asked her why she booed him during a tough loss:*

> "I didn't want anyone around me to know I knew you."

Dante Fedeli, *the coach of the women's softball team at Stanford University, after his team beat Mohegan Community College 56-39 in the opening game of the season:*

> "It was not a classic debut."

Comedian **Don Rickles,** *on Tommy Lasorda:*

> "He figures if the Dodgers blow the pennant again, he can tie a cord around his neck and work as a balloon."

Orioles pitcher **Jim Palmer,** *who never got along well with Earl Weaver, about new manager Joe Altobelli:*

> "The first time Joe said: 'Hello' to some guys, he broke Earl's career record."

Soft-spoken Dodgers coach **Joe Amalfitano,** *on the fact he was thrown out of only one game in 23 seasons:*

> "I suppose it's a nice record but they'll never ask me to do any beer commercials."

California Angels manager **Jim Fregosi,** *when asked if team owner Gene Autry considered him a son:*

> "Yes, an illegitimate one."

Billy Martin, *on the designated hitter rule:*

> "The National League voted unanimously to let the American League use it."

Milwaukee Brewers manager **Harvey Kuenn,** *talking about the bright side of having an artificial leg:*

> "It's the greatest thing that ever happened to me. Now I can park in all the best parking places."

Minnesota Twins manager **Billy Gardner,** *during a slump:*

> "Things are going so bad for me that if I bought a pumpkin farm they'd cancel Halloween."

Earl Weaver, *on why he came out of retirement:*

> "Economics had a lot to do with it. Cigarettes went up from $6.50 to $9.00 a carton."

Yogi Berra, *responding to 'Joe DiMaggio' when an interviewer asked him to play a word-association game:*

> "What about him?"

California Angels manager **Gene Mauch,** *after someone suggested his pitching staff resembled the one he managed in the 1965 all-star game:*

> "That's right, some are left-handed and some are right-handed."

Montreal Expos manager **Dick Williams:**

> "I only ask three things of my players — be at the park on time, don't make mental mistakes and give me the best you can give me on that particular day."

Sportscaster **Joe Garagiola,** *on Tommy Lasorda:*

> "You could plant two thousand rows of corn with the fertilizer he spreads around."

New York Mets manager **George Bamberger,** *an avid fisherman, during a losing streak:*

> "Don't talk to me about slumps. I haven't caught a fish in a long time. Now that's important stuff."

Hall of Fame pitcher **Warren Spahn,** *discussing the fact that he played for manager Casey Stengel early in his career and again late in his career:*

> "I knew Casey before and after he was a genius."

Baltimore Orioles slugger **Don Baylor,** *on the strategy employed by Earl Weaver:*

> "Earl likes good pitching, tight defence and three-run homers."

San Francisco Giants manager **Frank Robinson,** *when asked how he viewed the race in the National League's West Division:*

> "By looking up."

Seattle Mariners manager **Rene Lachemann,** *on what it's like to play Billy Martin and the Yankees:*

> "It's like a chess game. The only problem is when I look over to his dugout, he doesn't have too many pawns. He's got a lot of whatever you call those pieces that can go anywhere."

Los Angeles Dodgers pitcher **Jerry Reuss:**

> "The other day Tommy Lasorda held a team meeting and told us to forget about why we're not hitting and just go up there and let our bats do the talking. That night we got only two hits. The next day he told us our bats had laryngitis."

Boston Red Sox manager **Ralph Houk,** *when told that one sportswriter had picked his team to finish last in its division:*

> "Last? Who'd he pick ahead of us?"

Detroit Tigers manager **Sparky Anderson,** *when asked if he were going to push the panic button:*

> "Where would I push it?"

Yogi Berra, *after a waitress asked if he would like his pizza cut into eight slices or four:*

> "Better make it four. I don't think I can eat eight."

Jim Palmer, *talking about Earl Weaver:*

> "The only thing he knows about pitching is that he couldn't hit it."

Billy Martin, *on his dislike for the Hubert Humphrey Metrodome in Minneapolis:*

> "This place stinks. It's a shame a great guy like Hubert Humphrey had to be named after it."

Jerry Coleman, *after his release as manager of the San Diego Padres:*

> "I didn't ask them why they fired me, because I was afraid they might tell me."

Tommy Lasorda, *as the Dodgers went through customs:*

> "They've got dogs here trained to sniff out drugs and hotel towels, so be careful."

Cincinnati Reds coach **Bill Fisher,** *talking about a possible players' strike:*

> "This game is more than 100 years old. It has survived five wars. The German army and the Japanese army could not shut it down. Now, we're going to get it all messed up."

Bill Lee, *on former Montreal Expos manager Dick Williams:*

> "He had a little streak of Napoleon in him. And when he drank that cognac, he thought he was King Kong."

Chicago White Sox fan **Tiger Lyons:**

> "If you want to get rid of a skunk, try Tony LaRussa's warm-up jacket. He wore it for three weeks straight in the steamy heat during the Sox recent spurt."

Chicago Cubs pitching coach **Billy Connors,** *talking about his superstition during a slump:*

> "If we won the day before, I drive the same route to the ballpark. If we lost, I take a different route. Obviously, I've taken a lot of different routes this year. I could drive a cab I know the area so well. One time I ran out of gas because I had to go so far out of the way to find a different route."

Earl Weaver, *after a team meeting:*

> "It wasn't a meeting. It was a monologue and guess who did all the talking?"

Tacoma Tigers general manager **Stan Naccarato,** *after watching a fan reach up to catch a hard foul ball:*

> "If that ball had hit him in the head, he'd be dead for a month."

Yogi Berra:

> "I think Little League baseball is wonderful. It keeps the kids out of the house."

Los Angeles Dodgers manager **Walter Alston:**

> "He manages best who manages least."

Dodgers outfielder **Rick Monday,** *on manager Tommy Lasorda's tendency to swear after bad games:*

> "After we lose, you could put Tommy alone in a large room and he will verbally abuse all the paint off the wall in an hour."

Earl Weaver, *on why he smokes:*

> "They've got coupons on the back of the packages. I saved up one time and got Al Bumbry."

Gene Mauch, *on why he never reads anything other than sports publications:*

> "Ain't no boxscores in 'em."

Leo Durocher:

> "If I have to win one ball game, I want Jackie Robinson. But if I'm building a ball club, I want Pee Wee Reese."

Former major league umpire **Nestor Chylak,** *describing the managerial techniques of Billy Martin:*

> "Billy uses a system of play where you fight your own players, fight the other players, fight the owners, fight the press and fight strangers in a bar, and then, when you win, and someone wants to know the secret, you say: 'Teamwork.' "

California Angels third base coach **Preston Gomez:**

> "We have a different set of signs for every guy on the team. They don't know each other's signs and they don't need to know. All they need are their own. That way they don't get confused."

73

Texas Rangers manager **Don Zimmer,** *answering the clubhouse phone after his team snapped a 12-game losing streak:*

"Hello, is this President Reagan calling?"

Sparky Anderson:

"Don't make the role of the manager to be more than it is. When you get right down to it, the people who win the games are the ones out there on the field."

Minnesota Twins manager **Billy Gardner,** *on his modest lifestyle:*

"I've got hot runnin' water and cable TV. What more do you need?"

Oakland A's coach **Charley Metro,** *explaining why he nicknamed Harvey Kuenn 'Archie,' a name which stuck for more than 20 years:*

"He had just won the batting title and I didn't think the name Harvey was good enough for a batting champion."

Yogi Berra, *after the Yankees acquired his son Dale from Pittsburgh:*

"If he doesn't mind me, I'll tell his mother."

Kansas City Royals manager **Dick Howser:**

"Nobody takes getting beat as hard as a manager."

Kurt Bevacqua *of the San Diego Padres, on what it's like to play for Dick Williams:*

"It's like being the personal chef for Moammar Khadafy. Every meal better be good."

Earl Weaver, *when asked if he ever thought of himself as one of the greatest managers in baseball history:*

"Naw, all I think about is winning tonight so I can keep my job tomorrow. That's what it's all about."

Former Yankees manager **Gene Michael,** *when asked if he thought George Steinbrenner could manage the team:*

"I don't know but if he does, I want to be owner."

Tony LaRussa, *on one of his biggest problems as skipper:*

"Some of my players saw me play and know how bad I was."

BILLY MARTIN, AFTER YANKEE OUTFIELDER DAVE
WINFIELD KILLED A SEAGULL IN TORONTO;
"THAT'S THE FIRST TIME HE'S HIT THE
CUT-OFF MAN ALL SEASON."

Los Angeles Dodgers pitcher **Don Sutton,** *after someone described Tommy Lasorda as 'charitable':*

> "Yeah, every year he offers $50,000 to the family of the unknown soldier."

Kansas City Royals manager **Jim Frey,** *on spending 14 years in the minor leagues:*

> "When you're only 5'8", wear glasses, are a little overweight, have no power and don't throw well, it's a tough business."

Cleveland Indians manager **Pat Corrales,** *talking about a pitcher who throws everything from the stretch:*

> "We haven't told him he's a starter. We just tell him he's relieving the guy who finished up the night before, so he doesn't know the difference."

Jeff Albies, *baseball coach at William Paterson College in New Jersey, after his team had 10 games rained out early in the season:*

> "I don't even know what my players look like. All I do is hear their voices on the phone."

Billy Martin, *after he had thrown a temper tantrum in his office:*

> "I'm finally getting smarter. This time I didn't punch anything that could sue me."

Earl Weaver:

> "I used to carry a list of my managerial mistakes in my pocket but I had to stop — it gave me a limp."

Oklahoma State baseball coach **Gary Ward,** *commenting on his club's problems with weather:*

> "We opened the season in 80-degree weather in Nebraska. That's 80 degrees collectively — 27, 26, and 27 degrees."

Frank Robinson, *on charges that he could not communicate with players:*

> "I had no trouble communicating. The player just didn't like what I had to say."

Yogi Berra, *defending his habit of reading comic books:*

> "When I put 'em down, why does someone always pick 'em up?"

Dick Williams, *after showing the umpires three scuffed balls which had been used by the opposing pitcher:*

"I could have brought out six but I needed my other hand to talk with."

Earl Weaver, *on the William Penn Hotel:*

"That place is so old, I'm sure they named William Penn after the hotel."

Casey Stengel, *comparing two rookies:*

"See that fella there? He's 20 years old and in 10 years he's got a chance to be a star. Now that fella there, he's also 20 years old, and in 10 years he's got a chance to be 30."

Philadelphia Phillies manager **Paul Owens,** *when asked what the hardest part of managing is:*

"Standing up for nine innings."

Doug Rader, *after he was rejected as a major league manager because he didn't have any experience:*

"The Pilgrims didn't have any experience when they first arrived here. If experience was that important, we'd never have anybody walking on the moon."

New York Yankees outfielder **Dave Winfield,** *talking about Billy Martin:*

"Billy's style is to antagonize and intimidate. But he can't antagonize and intimidate me because I don't work for him, I'm not a marshmallow salesman, and what's more, if he needs a loan, he should call me for an appointment."

Philadelphia Phillies manager **Danny Ozark,** *when asked about his team's morale:*

"There's nothing wrong with this team's morality."

Chicago Cubs manager **Joey Amalfitano,** *after meeting newly-acquired outfielder Leon Durham:*

"I like his handshake. If that's any indication, he's going to do a great job for us."

Chicago Cubs manager **Leo Durocher:**

"Nice guys finish last."

Yogi Berra, *after leaving New York to join the Houston Astros:*

"Uniforms weigh the same. Some are just hotter than others."

Earl Weaver, *when asked if he had any physical problems:*

"Yeah, Jim Palmer."

Former major league manager **Bobby Bragan:**

"After you've managed players for a while, a sickness sets in. They get sick of you and you get sick of them."

Sparky Anderson, *talking about enforcing the team curfew:*

"I leave the hotel lobby just before the curfew. If I don't, I might see something I shouldn't."

Milwaukee Brewers manager **George Bamberger,** *following a game in which the Detroit Tigers pulled off a triple play:*

"That triple play took us right out of the inning."

Pittsburgh Pirates manager **Chuck Tanner:**

"The best feeling in the world is winning a big league game. The second-best feeling is losing a big league game."

Walter Alston, *after undergoing gall bladder surgery:*

"I played golf the other day and afterward I had a little blood on my shirt near where the incision is. I asked the doctor about it and he said: 'Don't worry — use cold water and it will come right out.' "

Gene Mauch, *on the strength of the game:*

"Baseball and malaria keep coming back."

California Angels manager **Jim Fregosi,** *on his ability to get along with his bosses:*

"My owners and I think exactly alike. Whatever they're thinking, that's what I'm thinking."

New York Mets manager **Joe Torre,** *explaining why the club signed Rusty Staub to a three-year contract at the age of 36:*

"He still says: 'Hey, I want to play,' instead of 'Aw, I got to play.' "

Manager **Birdie Tebbetts,** *to Bob Uecker before Uecker's first game:*

> "By the way, Bob, most of us wear our jocks inside our uniforms."

Yogi Berra:

> "If you ain't got a bullpen, you ain't got nothin'."

St. Louis Cardinals manager **Whitey Herzog,** *on his greatest achievement as a player:*

> "I once hit a line drive to pitcher Camilo Pascual, who threw to first baseman Julio Becquer, who relayed to shortstop Jose Valdivielso. So I'm the only guy in baseball history to hit into an all-Cuban triple play."

Dick Williams:

> "A lot of times I wear on people after a few years. But the person I worry most about I've been married to for 30 years. Then again, she doesn't ask me a lot of funny questions."

Earl Weaver, *arguing with Jim Palmer about his total number of wins:*

> "I'm only counting the ones you won since I've been here. The others don't count."

Dodgers outfielder **Rick Monday,** *on Tommy Lasorda:*

> "Cows may come and cows may go but the bull in this place goes on forever."

Oakland A's owner **Charlie Finley:**

> "Billy Martin is the first manager I ever had who didn't need my help."

CHAPTER 7

FOOTBALL PLAYERS

"He's like a diner, open all the time."

When **Herschel Walker** was a running back at the University of Georgia, he was continually faced with demands on his time. On one occasion, a wealthy and influential alumnus invited Herschel to have lunch with him at the fancy Peachtree Plaza. Walker did not want to seem ungrateful but he also wanted to protect his own privacy and free time.

"No, thank you, sir," he said. "I've already been there."

"Well, how about the Hyatt then?" pressed the alumnus.

"No, thank you, sir," replied Walker. "I've already been there."

"Then, how about Bugatti's?" insisted the alumnus.

"No, thank you, sir." said Walker. "I've already been there too."

Exasperated, the rich alumnus made one last attempt. "Then let's go to McDonald's, get a bag of hamburgers and eat them in the Clemson end zone. I know you've never been there."

Oakland Raiders defensive end **Lyle Alzado,** *when asked how tough he was:*

"Well, if King Kong and I went down an alley together, only one of us would come out and it wouldn't be the monkey."

Cleveland Browns placekicker **Lou Groza:**

"You never worry about missing a field goal. You just blame the holder and think about kicking the next one."

Houston Gamblers quarterback **Jim Kelly,** *when asked if he had any plans to get married:*
> "Just because you like milk doesn't mean you have to buy a cow."

Cincinnati Bengals receiver **Cris Collinsworth,** *on the advantages for single men of playing in the NFL:*
> "I've dated girls who were far better looking than the quality of girls who should be going out with me."

Cliff Stoudt, *after three seasons as back-up quarterback for the Pittsburgh Steelers:*
> "I've graduated from clipboards to headsets."

Bucknell University president **Dennis O'Brien,** *talking about the fact that many of the school's football players had helped freshmen move into the dorms by carrying trunks to the second and third floors:*
> "If we ever play on a field with a flight of stairs in the middle of it, we have a guaranteed victory."

Long Beach State defensive back **Scotty Byers,** *when asked his name after being knocked woozy:*
> "Who wants to know?"

Washington Redskins quarterback **Joe Theismann,** *talking about his role in a motion picture:*
> "I play a hood — takes me back to my childhood."

Miami Dolphins running back **Norm Bulaich,** *explaining how the fans pay tribute to him by using the first syllable of his last name:*
> "I'm the only guy to be cheered with a 'boo' but when I fumble you can always hear the 'oo' a little longer."

Miami Dolphins kicker **Garo Yepremian,** *when asked why he shaved off his moustache:*
> "My two boys were getting rashes when I kissed them."

University of Southern California quarterback **Paul McDonald,** *talking about his most embarrassing moment:*
> "At a crucial point in a high school game, I lined up behind the guard and started barking signals. Funny thing — the centre snapped the ball."

Former NFL player **Alex Hawkins,** *on his own level of courage:*

"I'm a devout coward."

Dallas Cowboys quarterback **Roger Staubach,** *after head coach Tom Landry had called several quarterback sneaks to run out the remaining time on the clock:*

"I wish you wouldn't call those plays, coach. You're ruining my rushing average."

Cleveland Browns rookie **Rich Dimler,** *when asked what he would do if he did not make the team:*

"If I'm cut, I'll go home to Bayonne (N.J.) and start my own team."

San Diego Chargers tight end **Kellen Winslow,** *when asked for the secret of his great pass-catching ability:*

"Dishpan hands. At my house, if you ate, you washed dishes. And I've been doing my own laundry since I was 12."

University of Southern California quarterback **Scott Tinsley:**

"Home is where your first stereo is."

Advertising representative **Penny Hawkey,** *describing the production problems in shooting a commercial which featured Joe Greene of the Pittsburgh Steelers:*

"Joe was a real trooper. We started shooting at seven in the morning and finished up by having Joe drink the Coke. He had to drink 18 16-ounce bottles in a row and he didn't even belch."

Chicago Bears safety **Doug Plank,** *talking about running back Larry Csonka of Miami:*

"I tried to tackle Larry around the ankles. But he was carrying so many of our men that I was afraid I might hit a teammate."

Jack Kemp, *describing how football prepared him for politics:*

"I had already been booed, cheered, cut, sold, traded and hung in effigy."

University of Cincinnati football coach **Ralph Staub,** *talking about University of Pittsburgh defensive end Hugh Green:*

"He isn't satisfied with just picking you up and putting you down. He wants to see how deep he can bury you."

Oklahoma linebacker **George Cumby,** *who was moved to defence after suffering three broken collarbones as a fullback:*

"I think they did it for my personal safety."

Winnipeg Blue Bombers quarterback **Kenny Ploen,** *on the 1962 'Fog Bowl' Grey Cup game:*

"The game was stopped after I threw a perfect pass — to referee Paul Dojack."

A defensive back at New York Tech, after his coach asked him why he 'froze' on one play, allowing the opposition to complete a 63-yard touchdown pass:

"I couldn't move, coach. My contact lens had just popped out and I covered it with my foot. If I had left that spot, I never would have found it again and my folks would have killed me."

Dallas Cowboys tackle **Pat Donovan,** *whose picture was on the tickets for a particular home game, after some 17,000 fans were no-shows:*

"Anyone else would be insulted but I choose to believe they are saving those tickets as collector's items."

Philadelphia Eagles linebacker **Anthony Griggs:**

"It's time to update football jargon. I'm not an outside linebacker, I'm an external enforcer. It's more new wave."

Oakland Raiders defensive lineman, **John Matuszak,** *on switching back and forth between defensive tackle and end:*

"I don't mind it. It's a change of pace. You get tired of smelling the same cologne all the time."

Cliff Stoudt, *after backing up Steelers quarterback Terry Bradshaw for three seasons:*

"If I play before the fourth game of the season, it will ruin my banquet jokes."

Former Pittsburgh Steelers centre **Ray Mansfield,** *on his relationship with linebacker Jack Lambert:*

> "I taught Jack a lot, like how to tie his shoes and how to brush his fangs."

Montreal Alouettes running back **John O'Leary,** *at his retirement:*

> "The doctors told me there are two things I can't do — play football and dive into empty swimming pools."

Nebraska Cornhuskers defensive tackle **David Clark:**

> "We're meaner than the Merrill Lynch bull."

Philadelphia Eagles back-up quarterback **Joe Pisarcik,** *about teammate Ron Jaworski:*

> "Ron got nailed against Chicago, they ran a brain scan and the doctors say it was the shortest brain scan in the hospital's history."

Cleveland Browns lineman **Bob Golic,** *describing his position:*

> "Playing nose tackle is like the opposite of Darwin's Theory, going from an upright, walking human being to a crawling, snivelling beast on all fours."

Syracuse University kicker **Gary Anderson,** *when asked how he felt about being watched by the Buffalo Bills:*

> "It's nothing new for me. I'm the son of a Baptist minister. I've had people watching me all my life."

Kansas State quarterback **Doug Bogue,** *explaining why he switched from veterinary medicine to petroleum geology:*

> "I didn't want any phone calls at 4 a.m. from people saying: 'FiFi is throwing up.' "

San Francisco 49ers tight end **Brian Billick,** *explaining why his playing career was so short:*

> "On my very first play, I lined up opposite Robert Brazile and all I could see were his forearms. I could hear him making those animal noises at me and I found I couldn't get out of my stance."

Los Angeles Raiders quarterback **Jim Plunkett:**

"We have only one rule on this team. Be on time for the games, if you can."

Chicago Bears locker room custodian **Dick McMurrin,** *after it was suggested that even he could play quarterback for the Bears:*

> "It's a heckuva lot more difficult being a janitor than being a quarterback. When it comes to carrying the garbage, I've got to carry it myself. I can't hand it off to a running back. And when I'm vacuuming the hallway, I don't have a platoon of blockers ahead of me."

Charlie Waters *of the Dallas Cowboys, explaining why teammate Aaron Mitchell's nickname is 'AM-PM':*

> "Because they're wide awake when he hits 'em and their lights are out when he walks away."

Texas Tech defensive lineman **Gabriel Rivera:**

> "Some days you feel like creaming somebody but other days you just feel like torturing them."

San Diego Chargers lineman **Louie Kelcher,** *explaining why he made a comeback after a 19-day retirement:*

> "You can only drink beer and listen to Willie Nelson for so long."

Jim Turner, *on his retirement as an NFL kicker:*

> "I guess I'll have to put up my shoes and let them collect some dust."

Cleveland Browns lineman **Doug Dieken,** *about Houston Oilers veteran Elvin Bethea:*

> "Elvin's so old he had to use a jumper cable to get started last year."

Lyle Alzado, *on a conversation he had with John Riggins of the Washington Redskins:*

> "I asked him if he was working out and he said: 'Yeah, I'm doing curls. I've got a Bud in one hand and a Miller in the other.' "

Western Mustangs quarterback **Jamie Bone,** *talking about a specific play during a game:*

> "I knew I was in trouble when we got to the line of scrimmage and I heard one running back say to the other: 'Who gets it — you or me?' "

New Orleans Saints centre **John Hill,** *talking about the debut of quarterback David Wilson:*

> "With most rookie quarterbacks, you can feel their hands shaking when they put them up under centre. Dave's hands didn't shake, he was loose."

Houston Oilers quarterback **Archie Manning,** *during the NFL players' strike:*

> "I miss football, even the interceptions."

Ball State University offensive lineman **Rick Chitwood,** *after injuries to teammates forced him to play all five positions along the offensive line:*

> "The toughest part was knowing where to stand in the huddle."

Washington Redskins quarterback **Sonny Jurgenson,** *on why he did not like rooming with linebacker Sam Huff:*

> "All he wanted to do was talk football."

Los Angeles Raiders tight end **Todd Christensen,** *on why he wears No. 46:*

> "Numbers show speed. You get in the secondary in zone coverage and they see 46. They know the guy's a stiff. He's a third-string white guy who can't run. He made the team because he makes tackles on kickoffs."

Chicago Bears safety **Doug Plank,** *explaining why he doesn't watch Monday Night Football:*

> "I'm afraid they'll show our highlights at halftime."

Roger Staubach, *explaining why he shaved off his moustache:*

> "Kids were coming up and asking if I was a kicker."

Wide receiver **John Jefferson,** *after being traded from San Diego to Green Bay, explaining the difference:*

> "One is on water that is flowing, the other on water that's about to freeze. One you water ski on, the other you ice skate on. Don't worry, I can learn to ice skate."

Joe Theismann, *talking about his Super Bowl preparations:*

> "I'm going to find a tough street where I can get beat up once a night. Then I'll be ready for the game."

Cecil Johnson *of the Tampa Bay Buccaneers, on playing linebacker in the NFL:*

"It's like walking through a lion's cage wearing a three-piece suit made of pork chops."

Former Seattle Seahawks wide receiver **Steve Raible:**

"Mine is the only jersey retired while I was still playing."

Denver Broncos quarterback **Craig Morton,** *who was never known for his speed, following a one-yard touchdown run:*

"Guard Tom Glassic really helped me out there. He blocked the same guy twice. He hit him once and then got up and hit him again when I came by."

Tom Harmon, *talking about the Heisman Trophy:*

"Nothing can touch it. It stands apart from the rest of the single outstanding awards in sports and those of us who won it are set apart as heroes beyond anything we ever dreamed possible. No other award could mean more to an athlete."

Green Bay Packers receiver **James Lofton,** *when asked to speculate on the remainder of the season:*

"Well, right now we're 2-5 with nine games left. That means we should finish somewhere between 11-5 and 2-14."

Steve Sabol *of NFL Films, when asked to name the best player he has seen in more than 30 years of watching football films:*

"The greatest was Dick Butkus. He was like Moby Dick in a goldfish bowl."

Veteran NFL guard **Conrad Dobler,** *after being accused of a cheap shot:*

"I didn't do anything. You ran into my arm and hurt your throat."

Hall of Fame quarterback **Otto Graham:**

"I would have played forever if it weren't for training camp."

FOOTBALL COACH JIM WALDEN, DESCRIBING
CHICAGO BEARS QUARTERBACK
JIM McMAHON:

"HE MAY BE THE BEST... GET-YOURSELF-OUT-OF-
A-MESS-AND-GET-SOMETHING-GOOD
QUARTERBACK I'VE SEEN IN A GOOD LONG TIME."

Dallas Cowboys wide receiver **Butch Johnson,** *when asked what he would do if he ever owned the team:*

"I would hire a coach who knows how to dance."

Sonny Jurgenson, *on his after-hours exploits:*

"Sam Huff said I was the most over-rated dissipater he ever roomed with. Maybe so but I never dissipated the night before a game."

Washington Redskins fullback **John Riggins,** *when asked which team he fears most:*

"The only team I fear is Nebraska. Fortunately, they're not on our schedule."

Notre Dame quarterback **Steve Beuerlein,** *talking about tough workouts at 6:15 a.m.:*

"Getting up at that hour is a pain. But I'll tell you one thing, seeing guys getting sick and throwing up really gives you a feeling of unity."

Former Los Angeles Rams defensive back **Don Burroughs,** *when asked how he remembers his tackles of Cleveland running back Jim Brown:*

"Every time I tackled him I could hear a dice game going on inside my mouth."

Joe Kapp, *explaining the problem he has with his German-Mexican heritage:*

"When I wake up in the morning, the German in me shouts: 'Achtung, let's get going.' But the Mexican in me says: 'Manana,' and I roll over and go back to sleep."

Dallas Cowboys linebacker **D.D. Lewis,** *on the moves of Pittsburgh running back Franco Harris:*

"He faked me out so bad one time I got a 15-yard penalty for grabbing my own facemask."

Former NFL running back **Gale Sayers,** *after winning the cow-chip throwing contest at the Duqoin, Ill., State Fair:*

"All I wanted to do was get the thing out of my hand."

University of Southern California quarterback **Scott Tinsley,** *a native of Oklahoma:*

> "My favorite part out here is the beaches. There aren't too many beaches in Oklahoma. Actually, there are lots of beaches in Oklahoma but no water."

New York Jets quarterback **Richard Todd,** *talking about the club's top draft choice, Ken O'Brien, another quarterback:*

> "He's a real nice guy — smart, strong, good arm, good-looking — all those things you hate to see. But I'd say he needs a little more training — like six or seven years."

Ted Hendricks *of the Los Angeles Raiders, when asked if he lifted weights to stay in shape for football:*

> "I lift but only so I don't look bad at the beach."

Dallas Cowboys quarterback **Danny White,** *on coach Tom Landry's plan to call plays from the sidelines:*

> "I told Tom to keep the shuttle system, sending in a player with the play. Then the one coming out could tell him what I really called."

Oakland Raiders kick returner **Ted Watts:**

> "Returning kicks is like embalming. Nobody likes to but somebody has to."

Anonymous voice from the back of the room, after the coach began training camp by saying: 'Okay, men, this is a football':

> "Please, coach, not so fast."

Detroit Lions coach, **Monte Clark,** *on the toughness of Miami fullback Larry Csonka:*

> "When he goes on safari, the lions roll up their windows."

Joe Theismann, *on how he learned to be a great scrambler:*

> "When you're a freshman at Notre Dame, they feed you to the starting defensive line in practice. Fear is a great motivator."

Gary Phillips, *Herschel Walker's high school football coach:*

> "We didn't coach Herschel, we just aimed him."

NFL guard **Joe DeLamielleure,** *on being a blue-collar kind of guy:*

> "Who else could be born in Detroit, drafted by Buffalo and traded to Cleveland? My only fear is that Gary, Ind., is going to get the next franchise."

Cliff Stoudt, *after three seasons as a back-up to Terry Bradshaw, during which he did not see any game action:*

> "I'm well-rested."

Former Los Angeles Rams running back **Dick Bass:**

> "The best three quarterbacks I ever saw couldn't count to 10. They always got stuck at eight."

Miami Dolphins quarterback **Bob Griese,** *on his retirement because of a shoulder injury:*

> "I'm like a gunslinger without a gun."

University of Washington tailback **Vince Coby,** *when asked to rate the top tailbacks in the Pac-10:*

> "Darrin Nelson at Stanford, Willie Gittens at Arizona State and all five of 'em at USC, whoever they are."

Tampa Bay Buccaneer **Dave Logan,** *on teammate Cecil Johnson:*

> "He's not the craziest person I know but he's definitely in the playoffs."

Quarterback **Joe Pisarcik,** *talking about the difference between starting for the lowly New York Giants and being a back-up with the promising Philadelphia Eagles:*

> "It's like being the president of a company that's going downhill, as opposed to being vice-president of a company that's doing well."

Dallas Cowboys running back **Tony Dorsett,** *after he picked up a total of eight yards on eight carries:*

> "Eight for eight. It sounds like I was coming to bat in the second game of a doubleheader."

Cleveland Browns quarterback **Paul McDonald,** *on the joys of throwing to receiver Ozzie Newsome:*

> "It's like throwing to an octopus who can run."

New York Jets running back **Freeman McNeil:**

"Some guys tilt, some guys are speed guys, some guys explode. I'm just a mutt runner — everything combined, whatever you throw in the trash and throw out in the bag."

Former NFL quarterback **Billy Kilmer,** *when asked what he named one of his racehorses:*

" 'Wobbly Pass.' "

CFL executive **Herb Capozzi:**

"Centres always have this strange little smile on their faces, a sort of uncertain look, which makes you wonder whether the quarterback has cold hands or what."

New York Giants linebacker **Harry Carson:**

"Linebackers are insane people. Our job, after all, is to give concussions to running backs."

Danny White, *on the possibility of being traded:*

"It's nice to know people are interested in you but you hate to think you're available."

Chicago Bears defensive tackle **Steve McMichael:**

"All the computers and all the genius coaches aren't worth a darn on Sunday if you don't have some tough guys who will go out and play like somebody just called their momma a bad name."

Texas Christian running back **Kenneth Davis,** *on the increase in football interest on campus:*

"The other students know our names and numbers now. They're more willing to approach us and offer to help us study."

Cleveland Browns lineman **Doug Dieken:**

"Being a nose tackle is like being the fire hydrant at a dog show."

Jack Kemp, *about his early years as a back-up quarterback:*

"I was the guy they kept around for insurance. They should have dressed me in a policy instead of a uniform."

Brigham Young University receiver **Glen Kozlowski,** *before his second straight appearance in the Holiday Bowl:*

> "Last year we got official Holiday Bowl watches. This year, the bowl has offered to fix the official Holiday Bowl watches."

Notre Dame coach **Knute Rockne:**

> "The only qualification for a lineman is to be big and dumb. To be a running back, you only have to be dumb."

Green Bay Packers tight end **Paul Coffman:**

> "I love playing in the snow. It slows everyone down to my speed."

Jimmy 'The Greek' Snyder, *on St. Louis receiver Roy Green:*

> "He's like a diner, open all the time."

Chicago Bears running back **Walter Payton,** *after a hard workout:*

> "I'm so sore, I can hardly turn on the television."

Cliff Stoudt, *after three seasons as a back-up quarterback:*

> "They almost put me on the disabled list at the Super Bowl. I had writer's cramp from charting plays."

A walk-on at the Atlanta Falcons training camp, when asked when he had last played football:

> "On which planet?"

Don Meredith:

> "I'd say the most important thing a quarterback can do is have his nerve endings removed. Hey, those are big guys hitting you and they hurt."

Vanderbilt defensive end **Glenn Watson,** *explaining why he changed his number from 92 to 36:*

> "I look a lot faster when I wear 36."

Roger Staubach, *at his retirement:*

> "I would like to be remembered as a pretty darn consistent performer."

CHAPTER 8

FOOTBALL COACHES

"Don't go to the Rolling Stones concert."

My **high school coach** played a big role in teaching me the value and importance of teamwork. One incident will always stand out.

It happened during the city championship game. We trailed by five points with less than a minute to play. Our offensive team was marching down the field for the possible winning touchdown. As a substitute player, I sat anxiously on the bench.

My coach was a bundle of nerves. He paced up and down the sidelines offering equal doses of encouragement, threats and pleas. As he did so, he kept glancing at me and somehow I sensed I would make a major contribution to this final drive.

Sure enough. With only seconds remaining and the ball inside the 10-yard line. . . .

"Price!" the coach shouted.

I hustled to his side, a million thoughts of heroism dashing through my mind.

"You understand, Gary, that every player on this team has a role to play."

"Yes, sir."

"And you understand that in order for this team to be successful, to become city champion, every player has to fulfill that role to the best of his abilities."

"Yes, sir."

"Are you ready to fulfill your role as a member of this team?"

"Yes, sir."

"All right, we need a time-out, so get in there and get hurt."

Arkansas coach **Lou Holtz,** *explaining his team's 'drop and roll' play:*

"First our quarterback drops back to pass and then he rolls out for his life."

Minnesota Vikings coach **Bud Grant:**

"A good coach needs a patient wife, a loyal dog and a great quarterback but not necessarily in that order."

University of Texas coach **Fred Akers:**

"Football does not take me away from my family life. We've always watched game films together."

University of Iowa coach **Hayden Fry,** *on the team's new uniforms:*

"We'll look a lot like the Pittsburgh Steelers — until the ball is snapped."

Indiana coach **Lee Corso,** *on the benefits of team speed:*

"The field shrinks for a team with speed. The first year we played Michigan, I felt we were playing on a postage stamp."

Calgary Stampeders coach **Jack Gotta,** *talking about the task ahead after the Stamps finished the 1976 season with only two wins:*

"I have a tough job in 1977. I can improve this club by 100 per cent and still finish last."

(It happened. The Stamps won four games in '77 and finished last.)

Houston Oilers coach **Bum Phillips,** *when asked if quarterback Ken Stabler could still throw deep:*

"Well, tell everybody to play real close and we'll find out."

Notre Dame coach **Dan Devine:**

"If I were to die now, I'd be leaving someone a pretty good team for the next two years."

University of Mississippi coach **Steve Sloan,** *after several of his veteran players suffered injuries:*

> "When the season opened, we had a bunch of old players and young coaches. Now we have a bunch of young players and old coaches."

Alabama coach **Bear Bryant,** *on the limit the NCAA imposes on the size of college coaching staffs:*

> "We simply don't have enough coaches to work with the junior varsity team any more. Now when you have a JV game, you just bundle them up, send them out to play and tell them not to get hurt."

Ohio State coach **Woody Hayes:**

> "Statistics always remind me of the fellow who drowned in a river which had an average depth of three feet."

Georgia Tech coach **Pepper Rodgers,** *explaining his progress midway through a season:*

> "We're an average football team. We were below average when the season started and now we're average."

Louisiana State coach **Jerry Stovall,** *talking about poor concentration:*

> "It's like kissing your girlfriend. You always try to kiss her on the lips but once in a while you might kiss her on the nose. Maybe you shut your eyes too soon. Well, that's a lack of proper concentration."

San Francisco 49ers coach **Bill Walsh:**

> "It's so important to have smart offensive linemen. If you've got a dumb one, you have to adjust all your blocking assignments to what he can remember."

Lou Holtz, *explaining the 'triple option' play:*

> "One back carries the ball, one back fumbles it and the third one is supposed to recover it."

Dorothy Shula, *wife of Miami Dolphins coach Don Shula:*

> "I'm fairly confident that if I died tomorrow, Don would find a way to preserve me until the season was over and he had time for a nice funeral."

Anonymous coach:

"I demand one thing from my players and that's a positive attitude. I want them to think as positively as the 85-year-old man who married a 25-year-old woman and bought a five-bedroom house near an elementary school."

Kansas State coach **Jim Dickey:**

"We've played in so many Homecoming games that our players are going to start judging floats."

Baylor coach **Grant Teaff,** *after his Bears broke a losing streak:*

"I hadn't smiled in so long my facial muscles had atrophy."

Notre Dame coach **Knute Rockne:**

"You can't be a football player and a lover too."

Cleveland Browns coach **Sam Rutigliano,** *on why he decided not to have his players look at game films of a bad loss:*

"I don't believe in pornographic films."

High school coach **Ron Marciel:**

"We started throwing the ball well last year. If we can catch it this year we should be okay."

Vanderbilt coach **George MacIntyre,** *talking about the large number of freshmen on his team:*

"Our biggest concern is diaper rash."

University of Arizona coach **Tony Mason,** *on what it's like to compete for players with John Robinson of Southern Cal:*

"I sell cactus, he sells Heismans."

Houston Oilers coach **Bum Phillips:**

"When I die, I want you to put on my tombstone: 'He would have lived a lot longer if he hadn't played the Pittsburgh Steelers six times in two years.' "

Auburn coach **Shug Jordan:**

"A young coach works players until they're exhausted, while an old coach works players until he's exhausted."

Arizona Wranglers coach **Doug Shively:**
> "Asking Herschel Walker to block is like asking Liberace to carry the piano."

University of Illinois coach **Mike White,** *on recruiting:*
> "We met some resistance. Illinois does not have the state-wide image I thought it had."

Bear Bryant, *following his 323rd coaching victory, the one which set a record:*
> "Whether the players like it or not, whether I like it or not, people will remember this game."

Texas-El Paso coach **Bill Yung,** *describing how badly things had gone for his team:*
> "My strong safety hurt his shoulder in the locker room raising his arm to say: 'Charge!' "

Cincinnati Bengals coach **Forrest Gregg,** *during the NFL players' strike:*
> "This is what hell must be like — spending all your time working up a game plan and never playing the game."

Lou Holtz:
> "Our kicking game is still a big question mark. You'll probably see better kicking at the finals of the Punt, Pass and Kick competition."

Mrs. Jack Pardee, *on why she never worried when her husband was fired by the Washington Redskins:*
> "Jack can do anything well. If Jack has to dig ditches, they'll be the best ditches in the world."

Bud Elliott, *coach at Texas-Arlington, after his team gave up 121 points in three games:*
> "I don't know if I'd want our defence protecting my house."

Green Bay Packers coach **Vince Lombardi:**
> "Football is, and always will be, a running game first."

Tampa Bay Buccaneers coach **John McKay:**
> "A football genius is the coach who won last Sunday."

Sportswriter **Dick Otte,** *about Ohio State coach Woody Hayes:*

"Woody doesn't have many faults but he makes the most of the ones he has."

Los Angeles Rams defensive end **Fred Dryer,** *talking about the nervous habits of defensive coordinator Bud Carson:*

"Old Bud takes a carton of cigarettes and plays it like a harmonica."

Lou Holtz, *on time-of-possession stats:*

"The only important thing about time-of-possession is who gets to keep the ball after the game."

Bum Phillips:

"There are only two ways to build a strong football team. You either get better players, or you get the players you've got to be better players."

Florida State coach **Bobby Bowden,** *on why he turns down invitations to go on alumni fishing trips:*

"After the season we had last year, it might not be a good idea for me to get in a boat with some of our alumni."

Atlanta Falcons coach **Leeman Bennett:**

"We're not blessed with an overabundance of great football violinists but we are blessed with 45 fiddlers who play beautiful music."

Detroit Lions coach **Monte Clark,** *giving his team three days off:*

"Just don't do anything dangerous like skiing, snowmobiling, or going to the Rolling Stones concert."

Hamilton Tiger-Cats coach **George Dickson:**

"I really believe if a man is a quarterback, he should call the plays. However, I think he should also get some help from the sidelines. But if he gets himself into a second-and-25 situation, he's not getting any help from me."

Kansas State coach **Jim Dickey,** *on the new lights at the stadium — lights mounted on poles which rise 160 feet into the air:*

"The first guy who drops a pass, fumbles, or misses a tackle has to go up and change a light bulb."

Notre Dame coach **Dan Devine:**

"A team is a team is a team. Shakespeare said that lots of times."

Georgia Tech coach **Pepper Rodgers,** *when asked what he wanted his epitaph to read:*

"Pepper Rodgers was a terrible recruiter but he overcame it with great coaching."

Lou Holtz, *describing his preferences in athletic competition:*

"Let me put my loyalties on record. Whenever anyone from Arkansas is playing, I always pull for that team. When an Arkansas school isn't involved, I'm for the Southwest Conference. If a league school is not involved, I'm for the United States. If our country is not involved, I'm for the universe."

Houston Oilers coach **Bill Peterson,** *admitting he has trouble remembering names:*

"I'm better, though, since I took that Sam Carnegie course."

Woody Hayes, *to a reporter:*

"Don't write anything nice about me. I might have to live up to it."

Vanderbilt coach **George MacIntyre,** *when asked to assess his recruits:*

"It's impossible. The only thing I know for sure is the linemen are ugly and the receivers are pretty."

Florida A&M coach **Jake Gaither,** *talking about Bear Bryant:*

"The Bear can take his and beat yours and take yours and beat his."

Anonymous Chicago Bears fan:

"Good news and bad news. First the bad news, some thieves broke into the coach's car. The good news, they stole the Bears' game plan."

Head coach at a Roman Catholic school:

"Like all coaches, I'm optimistic at the beginning of a season. And righteously so."

Joe Salem, *after he resigned as coach at the University of Minnesota:*

> "It's important in retirement that you find something to do each day like go to breakfast with Sam or out to lunch with Dick. But just make sure you don't go out to lunch and breakfast on the same day. Otherwise, you won't have anything to do the next day."

Houston Oilers coach **Jerry Glanville,** *talking about all the moves he has had to make during his career:*

> "I've got the kind of furniture that, when you snap your fingers, it jumps into the crates."

Lou Holtz, *on why he chose defensive end Billy Ray Smith to kick field goals:*

> "Billy misses closer than the other guys."

Boston College coach **Reid Oslin,** *after his school agreed to meet Notre Dame in the Liberty Bowl:*

> "We are the only Catholic schools still playing Division 1-A. Maybe we should have a bingo game at halftime."

Bum Phillips:

> "Sure I know what a three-piece suit is. That's overalls with two straps."

UCLA coach **Terry Donahue,** *when asked about the effect of smog on his practices:*

> "I don't acknowledge smog, it hurts recruiting."

Dallas Cowboys coach **Tom Landry,** *responding to praises that he has been the only coach in the team's history:*

> "That's one way to look at it. The other is that I haven't had a promotion in 21 years."

Tampa Bay coach **John McKay,** *when he learned that both he and Bear Bryant would be in Dallas for playoff games on the same weekend:*

> "Bear and I in the same town? I don't think Dallas is big enough for both of us."

New York Jets coach **Walt Michaels:**

> "Everyone has some fear. A man who has no fear belongs in a mental institution, or on special teams."

Grambling coach **Eddie Robinson:**

> "When the boys get in trouble and are told they can make one phone call, they always phone me."

Jim Dickey, *when asked if bad field position hurt his team in a loss:*

> "No, I had good field position. I stood on the 50-yard line all day."

Coach, when asked if his team has a pre-game prayer:

> "No, we've got so many things to pray for we'd get penalized 15 yards for delay of game."

Lou Holtz, *talking about drugs in sports:*

> "We've got to do more to get rid of the drug problem in sports. And when we get rid of pot and drugs, then we've got to work on Pac-Man."

Bum Phillips, *on the Dallas Cowboys:*

> "They have a little sputter like an auto on a cold morning. But they usually crank up and it runs good after it cranks up."

Cincinnati Bengals defensive lineman **Mike White,** *on the coaching he received at college:*

> "All they said was 'run, run, run — beat, beat, beat — kill, kill, kill!' When I got here, I didn't know a lot."

Oklahoma coach **Barry Switzer,** *on why his school has a recruiting edge on Oklahoma State:*

> "'OU' is easier to spell than 'OSU.' "

Bear Bryant, *after his record 323rd victory:*

> "We won the game in spite of me. Actually, I hardly knew what we were doing. I don't recall making an important decision all night."

Woody Hayes, *giving advice to his players:*

> "When we get to winning and someone comes up to congratulate you, kick 'em in the shins, unless it's a little old lady over 80. Pats on the back soften you."

Miami Dolphins coach **Don Shula:**

> "Sure, luck means a lot in football. Not having a good quarterback is bad luck."

Pittsburgh coach **Chuck Noll,** *when asked if the Steelers could be considered a dynasty after they won their fourth Super Bowl title in six years:*

> "Dynasty? Isn't that someplace you eat?"

University of Miami coach **Howard Schnellenberger,** *on the advantages of his long name:*

> "You get more ink (newspaper coverage) when you've got a long name."

Mrs. Bob Tyler, *whose husband was the head coach at Mississippi State, on what it's like to be a coach's wife:*

> "It's like being co-pilot to a Kamikaze pilot."

San Francisco 49ers coach **Bill Walsh:**

> "It's not so much a matter of what plays you use as how you use your players."

University of Minnesota coach **Lou Holtz,** *on recruiting:*

> "What I'm looking for is a running back who can carry the ball 20 times on Saturday and then show up at practice Monday without a lawyer, doctor or agent."

Ball State coach **Dwight Wallace,** *when he learned that the 'player of the year' in the mid-American Conference would be given an expensive glass sculpture:*

> "I hope they don't give it to one of my receivers."

Texas-El Paso coach **Bill Yung,** *describing how his team was preparing for powerful Southern Methodist:*

> "We're going to take the SMU players to Rose's Cantina and let them drink gringo water. That'll give them he areba mebas."

Monte Clark, *explaining why he hired a new assistant coach after a 2-14 season:*

"Some changes were needed."

High school coach **Al Antak,** *after one of his players ran 54 yards the wrong way:*

"We need to start teaching geography a few years earlier."

University of Minnesota coach **Lou Holtz,** *when asked what his team's chances of success were entering the 1984 season:*

"We have a better shot than Richard Nixon does of becoming president but probably not as good as Jesse Jackson."

Kansas City Chiefs coach **John Mackovic,** *describing the difference between today's athletes and those of the past:*

"In the old days we coaches would say: 'Go over and stand in the corner.' That evolved into: 'Please stand in the corner.' Then it became: 'How about we talk about your standing in the corner.' Now we have to say: 'Why don't I go over and stand in the corner for you?' "

Anne Hayes, *when asked if she ever gave advice to her husband Woody:*

"I'd never tell Woody what to do. I don't believe it's a woman's place to tell her husband how to run his job. I can't stand it when a woman tries to impose her will on her husband. There's no place in the world for that kind of thing. I'd just pass more often."

Louisiana State coach **Jerry Stovall,** *on his team's lack of experience:*

"They have 24 players who are married. We don't have 24 players old enough to date."

Notre Dame coach **Dan Devine,** *responding to someone who said coaching the Fighting Irish had to be the third toughest job in the U.S., behind the president and the mayor of New York City:*

"How did the mayor get in there?"

Arizona State offensive line coach **Tom Freeman,** *on the severity of mental mistakes:*

"It is better to die at birth than jump offside at the goal line."

George Allen, *as coach of the Chicago Blitz in the U.S. Football League:*

> "We have territorial rights to Red Grange. He's 81 years old and living in Boca Raton. We'll use him on third-and-one situations."

Kansas State quarterback coach **Darrel Dickey:**

> "I try to teach them the things that aren't in the playbook — how to walk off the field after an interception, how to dodge whiskey bottles thrown from the stands, how to find the back door of the dressing room."

Rice University coach **Ray Alborn,** *explaining why he doesn't judge his players in spring workouts:*

> "Spring workouts are a lot like spring flowers. They're all pretty and look real nice but when the fall rolls around they aren't worth a darn."

Lou Holtz, *after joining the University of Minnesota:*

> "Since I've been here, there have only been three different weather reports — bitterly cold, unbearably cold and unbelievably cold."

Florida State coach **Bobby Bowden,** *talking about one of his linebackers:*

> "He doesn't know the meaning of the word 'fear.' In fact, I just saw his grades and he doesn't know the meaning of a lot of words."

Mississippi State coach **Emory Bellard,** *assessing Nebraska:*

> "Well, we can isolate their strengths down to their offence, defence and kicking game. Their uniforms are nice too but actually they're pretty routine in that regard."

Canisius coach **Tom Hershey,** *talking about the high intelligence of one of his players:*

> "I mean, he's so intelligent, it's hard to communicate with him, his being so intelligent and trying to talk to a dumber guy like myself."

Running back **Archie Griffin,** *talking about Woody Hayes:*

> "Woody is a little behind in his knowledge of the drug culture. He still thinks 'uppers' are dentures."

Hamilton Tiger-Cats coach **George Dickson:**

> "My wife doesn't know much about football and that's the way I like it. If she ever starts to second-guess me, she'll soon be on some other team."

Arkansas State coach **Larry Lacewell,** *after he was told placekicker Jim Hatfield would play in a game despite a stress fracture in his lower back.*

> "This is the first time I've had a placekicker who could play with pain. Most of them play with passports."

Duquesne coach **Don McCann,** *talking about Georgetown placekicker Jim Corcoran, who played key roles in beating his team three years in a row:*

> "I'm going to attend his graduation just to be sure he's gone."

Houston Oilers coach **Bum Phillips,** *after his team lost its second straight AFC championship to the Pittsburgh Steelers:*

> "Last year, we knocked on the door. This year, we beat on the door. Next year, we're gonna kick it in."

Los Angeles Rams coach **John Robinson,** *on the intense competition for jobs at every position:*

> "I'm not sure if we have great depth, or two terrific second-teams."

Lou Holtz:

> "The man who complains about the way the ball bounces is likely the one who dropped it."

Stanford coach **Paul Wiggins,** *talking about a play in which an opposing ball carrier had to run through the Stanford band to score a touchdown:*

> "The same thing won't happen next time. We have the trombone section of our band working out in the weight room."

John Robinson, *describing his game plan with Eric Dickerson back in the Rams line-up:*

> "Eric around right end, Eric around left end, Eric up the middle."

Vanderbilt coach **George MacIntyre,** *on his pre-season strategy to motivate one of his players:*

> "He's the kind of guy who improves a lot as the season goes on. So I've informed him we've already played seven games."

Minnesota Vikings coach **Les Steckel,** *on what it's like to be a head coach in the NFL:*

> "It's like being pregnant. You don't understand it until you go through it."

New England Patriots coach **Ron Meyer,** *talking about his enthusiastic players:*

> "Heck, enthusiasm isn't enough. The Americans had all kinds of enthusiasm at the Alamo but the execution was awful."

Cleveland Browns coach **Sam Rutigliano,** *on running back Mike Pruitt:*

> "Pruitt's like Swiss cheese. He has to have the holes."

Politician **Eugene McCarthy:**

> "A football coach has to be smart enough to understand the game and dumb enough to think it's important."

Lou Holtz, *commenting on his club's defensive problems:*

> "Any time your defence gives up more points than the basketball team, you're in trouble."

University of California coach **Joe Kapp,** *talking about a new defensive end:*

> "He eats garlic and likes to hang out around quarterbacks."

Sportswriter **Dick Otte,** *at a roast for Woody Hayes:*

> "Woody grew up to be the man his father told him not to associate with."

CHAPTER 9

BASKETBALL PLAYERS

"Young man, you have the question backward."

Basketball players have to be quick and agile on the court and sometimes even off the court.

During a Philadelphia 76ers road trip, coach Billy Cunningham told his players that practice the next day was set for 10 to 11. At 10 the next morning, rookie **Marc Iavaroni** was missing. Iavaroni finally arrived at precisely 10:50 and received a stern lecture on punctuality from Cunningham.

But Iavaroni, either by design or by accident, had the perfect comeback.

"I don't know what you're yelling about, coach," he protested. "You said practice was 10 to 11 and that's exactly what time I got here."

Atlanta Hawks general manager **Stan Kasten,** *on Larry Bird of the Boston Celtics:*
"The guy came down to the NBA from a higher league."

Julius Erving *of the Philadelphia 76ers, responding to a comment that he always kept one eye on the basket and one eye on his man:*
"I always keep both eyes on my man. Heck, the basket hasn't moved on me yet."

Washington Bullets trainer **John Lally,** *on Elvin Hayes:*
"For some of us, being around Elvin every day is like Chinese water torture. It's just a drop at a time, nothing big but in the end he drives you crazy."

Philadelphia 76ers centre **Darryl Dawkins,** *after he played a game with electrodes taped to his shoulder to ease the pain:*

"They affected my interplanetary funksmanship."

Dave Huffman, *who left his home state of Texas to play basketball at Notre Dame:*

"I didn't want to go where everyone I'd meet would be from Sweetwater or Magnolia Tree or Frogs Knot or whatever. I thought I was coming to the big city and I got South Bend."

Seattle SuperSonics guard **Gus Williams,** *after playing in the NBA all-star game:*

"The game was fine but I was just as excited by the other things associated with the game — like the media coverage and the San Diego Chicken."

New York Knicks star **Bill Bradley,** *on why he passed up offers to do TV commercials:*

"Basketball was an important part of my life. I wanted to keep it pure. I cared about basketball but hair sprays and deodorants and popcorn poppers were not basketball."

New Orleans Jazz star **Pete Maravich,** *when asked if he were willing to play second-fiddle to Kareem Abdul-Jabbar in the event he was traded to the Los Angeles Lakers:*

"Are you kidding? I'll be his caddy. I'll take his clothes to the laundry. I'll pick him up and drive him around. If it meant winning a championship ring, I'd be happy to be a zero scorer."

Virginia Tech player **Les Henson,** *after he sank an 89-foot shot at the buzzer to give his team a two-point victory:*

"At first I thought it was going to hit the lights but it just kept going and going. When it went through, I turned to a Florida State cheerleader and said: 'Can you believe that shot?' "

Guard **Lynn Norenberg** *of William and Mary University, before a game against a strong opponent:*

"They're no different from anyone else. They put on their bras just like we do."

Denver Nuggets centre **Rich Kelley,** *commenting on a rumor he would be traded to Cleveland:*

> "That would be followed shortly by the announcement of my retirement."

Junior Bridgeman *of the Milwaukee Bucks, after he was credited with 10 rebounds in a playoff game:*

> "It helps when you pay the statistician $5 for every rebound he gives you."

Billy Paultz *of the Houston Rockets, on the difficulty of making the NBA playoffs:*

> "It's not as challenging now that they've expanded the playoffs. All you have to do is make a team in the fall, and still be breathing in the spring, and you're in."

Kiki Vandeweghe, *who worked as a sportscaster during the off-season, opening his show on the day he was traded by the Denver Nuggets:*

> "In the top story of the day, I've been traded to Portland."

Boston Celtics guard **Danny Ainge,** *acknowledging his reputation as a complainer on the court:*

> "I've checked into 'Wailers Anonymous' for rehabilitation."

Los Angeles Lakers forward **James Worthy,** *after a bad loss:*

> "Our performance was miraginal. We were seeing things that weren't there."

New Jersey Nets coach **Stan Albeck,** *talking about injury-prone Bill Walton of San Diego:*

> "He's incredible. If you drop a toothpick on his foot, he'll have a stress fracture."

Mychal Thompson *of the Portland Trail Blazers, talking about his coach Jack Ramsay:*

> "He's a maniac and I mean that as a compliment."

Boston Celtics forward **M. L. Carr:**

> "Talking is half my game."

Darryl Dawkins:

> "After all is said and done, there's nothing left to say or do."

111

Los Angeles Lakers guard **Magic Johnson,** *talking about teammate Kareem Abdul-Jabbar:*

"In tight games we say: 'Please, big fella, save us.' "

Mitchell Wiggins *of the Chicago Bulls, discussing his dislike for the elements in the 'Windy City':*

"I'm not too hot on cold weather."

Atlanta Hawks guard **Glenn Rivers,** *on driving the lane against imposing Moses Malone of Philadelphia:*

"I'm from Chicago. I'm not scared of anything."

Cleveland Cavaliers centre **Edgar Jones:**

"You're only as good as your limitations and I don't have any."

New Jersey Nets centre **Mike Gminski,** *after his team took the lead in a playoff series against highly-favored Philadelphia:*

"I'd have to eat pizza at midnight to dream something like this."

Boston Celtics coach **Bill Fitch,** *describing Philadelphia guard Andrew Toney:*

"When Toney's got it going, it's like Liberace at the piano. It doesn't matter whether the candles are lit or not because he can play in the dark."

Kansas State forward **Ed Nealy,** *on his philosophy of rebounding:*

"I always figure the ball is yours until somebody can take it away."

Utah Jazz coach **Frank Layden,** *talking about the range of intelligence among NBA players:*

"At one end was Tom McMillen of Atlanta, a Rhodes Scholar. At the other end was a guy who shall remain nameless. We got a pretty good reading on him when we looked at the information sheet he filled out for our PR department. On the line where 'church preference' was requested, the guy wrote: 'Red brick.' "

Rich Kelley *of the Sacramento Kings, on what he has learned during his many years in the NBA:*

> "How to take naps. There are very few NBA players who can't fall asleep between 3 and 5 p.m. on the day of a game."

Larry Bird, *on why he refuses to talk about his private life:*

> "My private life is nobody's business, and besides, it ain't interesting."

Former NBA star **Wilt Chamberlain,** *suggesting how the New York Knicks could increase their attendance:*

> "Bring me in at halftime, let me shoot 20 foul shots and take bets on whether I can make five."

Marvin Barnes, *who was always in trouble during his NBA career:*

> "If there's such a thing as reincarnation, I'd like to come back as a wrestler — someone like Andre the Giant. Then, finally, people would look at me as a good guy."

Kenny Dennard *of the Denver Nuggets, on playing against Michael Jordan of Chicago:*

> "Covering him is like trying to cover the space shuttle."

John Johnson *of the Seattle SuperSonics, when he was released after 12 years in the NBA:*

> "Am I eligible for unemployment?"

Former NBA centre **John Kerr,** *when asked how he would try to cover Lakers centre Kareem Abdul-Jabbar:*

> "I'd get really close to him and breathe on his goggles."

Notre Dame guard **Larry Williams,** *on the pressure to win:*

> "At other schools, hope springs eternal. Here, demand springs eternal."

Los Angeles Lakers guard **Michael Cooper,** *on the lack of recognition given to defensive players:*

> "They should have a stat called 'FB' — floor burns. Defensive players are like garbage collectors. They handle the messes and the stinky stuff."

Ohio State forward **Clark Kellogg,** *talking about Northwestern:*

> "They've got a strong team. They just don't score enough points to out-total the opposition."

Linnel 'Magic' Jones *of the St. Louis Streak in the Women's Professional Basketball League:*

> "The WBL is great. It gives women like me who don't want to work something to do."

Sportswriter **Mike Littwin,** *about a certain player:*

> "He thought he was in the biathlon. Every time he stopped, he shot."

Illinois State star **Mark Herron,** *on the weather in the Midwest:*

> "It's so cold you have to jump-start reindeer."

Darryl Dawkins, *on Thanksgiving:*

> "I would have been a great pilgrim. Tell you one thing, I would have steered that ship (Mayflower) to the right place, not into those rocks. I probably would have skipped America and set sail straight for Hawaii."

Lee Goza *of Georgia Tech, who accidentally scored a basket for North Carolina:*

> "Sure wish momma could have seen this one. She always wanted me to score for North Carolina."

Georgia State player **Mark Gulmire,** *after he filled in on the golf team and fired a 117:*

> "I always try to be the high scorer on every team I play for."

Denver Nuggets centre **Dan Issel,** *on his team's offence:*

> "We fast break when it's available and we fast break when it's not available and we fast break at halftime."

An anonymous fan, after Golden State selected 7'8" Chibi Okayama of Osaka, Japan in the eighth round of the NBA draft:

> "He must have been the best player available."

Former NBA great **Bill Russell,** *when asked by a reporter how he would fare against Kareem Abdul-Jabbar:*

> "Young man, you have the question backward."

Sportswriter **Steve Kelley,** *on Ray Tolbert of the Seattle SuperSonics:*

"Some nights he's a turnover waiting to happen."

San Diego Clippers centre **James Donaldson,** *on his parents' lack of interest in basketball:*

"They just found out that Magic Johnson and Dr. J aren't the same person."

Bill Walton, *when asked if he had dropped any places from his list of possible places to play next year:*

"Yeah, Tehran and Three Mile Island."

Larry Bird, *on former teammate Rick Robey:*

"I always invite Robey to my summer basketball camp so the kids can see for themselves what not to do. The kid who plays most like Robey gets a free scholarship to next year's camp."

Phoenix Suns centre **Alvan Adams,** *trying to explain to his coach why he missed a practice:*

"I was attending the funeral of my butcher."

Caldwell Jones *of the Philadelphia 76ers, when someone suggested the only way to stop teammate Andrew Toney was to lock him out of the gym:*

"That wouldn't stop him. He'd still make 15 or 20 through the keyhole."

Boston Celtics coach **Bill Fitch,** *on one of his more talkative players:*

"He may be the first player I've ever had who had to get his tonsils taped."

Jimmy Black *of North Carolina University, when asked about the Georgetown defence:*

"I haven't seen Georgetown play. I don't like to watch college basketball."

Buck Williams *of the New Jersey Nets, explaining why he doesn't get many assists:*

"I know I have teammates out there somewhere. I just don't know where."

Atlanta Hawks guard **Spud Webb,** *who is only 5'7", when asked why he drives the lane so often against much taller opponents:*

"That's where the basket is."

Billy Paultz, *on the advantages of playing pro basketball:*

"The hours are good, the pay is good, for the most part you meet good people, you stay in shape, you get summers off and sometimes you even get your name in the papers."

Dallas Mavericks reserve forward **Charlie Sitton,** *after playing for two seconds in a victory over Portland:*

"It was nice to be out there long enough to get a feel for the game."

San Diego Clippers forward **Terry Cummings,** *on growing up as one of 13 children:*

"Our family was big enough to be our own gang."

New York Knicks forward **Bob Thornton,** *on how it felt to get a punch in the face during an altercation with an opponent:*

"Like Mr. Spock doing the Vulcan mind probe."

Darryl Dawkins:

"I once jumped off the house when I was 11. I'd just seen 'Mary Poppins' and I thought I could fly. I almost broke my neck and I got a beating for breaking an umbrella."

Lafayette Lever *of the Portland Trail Blazers, on the team's offensive system:*

"It's so complicated even some of the veterans don't know the plays. Either you have to know what you're doing, or be great at faking it."

Mark Landsberger *of the Los Angeles Lakers, to a teammate about to pick up the Wall Street Journal:*

"Don't bother. Somebody already swiped the sports section."

University of Southern California star **Cheryl Miller,** *comparing men's and women's basketball:*

"We're doing everything like men except shaving."

Rich Kelley, *when a Hare Krishna disciple asked for a donation:*

"I gave in another life."

Kings guard **Reggie Theus,** *after he was traded from the Chicago Bulls, on the slower pace of life in Kansas City:*

"I admit there's no Rush Street here but if I get really bored I can drive to Omaha."

John Johnson *of the Seattle SuperSonics, on teammate Gus Williams:*

"He's the only guy I know who's got seven cars and still needs a ride everywhere."

Julius Erving:

"I've got the greatest job in the world. If I weren't doing this for a living, I'd likely be playing a couple of nights a week at the 'Y' and getting all these bumps and bruises for free."

San Diego Clippers centre **Swen Nater:**

"Some people say I'm a dirty player. I'm not a dirty player. I take lots of showers."

Elvin Hayes *of the Washington Bullets, on the fact that Moses Malone won the league's MVP award:*

"He can win all the MVPs he wants as long as he has an early summer vacation and I'm in the battle for the league title."

University of Virginia star **Ralph Sampson,** *when asked what athletic awards he had won:*

"Lots."

Paul Westphal *of the Seattle SuperSonics, on the value of teammate Wally Walker:*

"He is the second most important player on our team. He's the guy who drives Jack Sikma to the games."

Sly Williams, *fringe guard in the old American Basketball Association and NBA:*

"If I ever get another chance to play in this league, I'm going to revolutionize this game."

Boston Celtics coach **Bill Fitch,** *on the one problem he has with Danny Ainge, a former baseball player with the Toronto Blue Jays:*

"I can't ever scratch my nose during a game. Ainge still thinks it's a bunt sign."

Classical pianist **Russell Sherman,** *talking about the efficient play of Washington Bullets forward Jeff Ruland:*

"He's like a good bassoon player. He doesn't have much to do but he knows exactly when to come in and do it and when to leave."

Seattle SuperSonics coach **Lenny Wilkens,** *after injury-prone Bill Walton joined the San Diego Clippers:*

"He's going to get their Medicaid rates up."

Los Angeles Lakers coach **Paul Westhead,** *on Jamaal Wilkes:*

"He plays the game quietly, like snow falling off a bamboo leaf."

George Underwood, *of East Tennessee State:*

"I've got two superstitions. First, don't call someone stupid if he's got a loaded pistol, and second, don't call your girlfriend Tina if her name is Vivian."

Rich Kelley, *on how he was able to play 11 seasons without serious injury:*

"My game is very horizontal. That's why I've never had any knee problems. Knees like horizontal players."

Chicago Bulls trainer **Mark Pfeil,** *on what it means to the team to play without injured Michael Jordan:*

"The valuables bag is a lot lighter."

Atlanta Hawks PR man **Bill Needle,** *talking about guard Eddie Johnson who had returned to the line-up on separate occasions from being shot, being arrested for drug possession and undergoing psychiatric treatment for a manic-depressive personality:*

"The only thing left for Eddie to come back from is pregnancy."

119

Caldwell Jones *of the Philadelphia 76ers, on the difference between playing Larry Bird and Kareem Abdul-Jabbar:*

> "Covering Bird, my legs are worn out. Covering Kareem, my elbows are worn out."

Dan Issel *of the Denver Nuggets, on the phone to his wife just before boarding a team flight which had been delayed by a bomb threat:*

> "If you hear a big explosion over Denver in about 20 minutes, the insurance policy is in the second drawer."

Darryl Dawkins, *on why he wears No. 53:*

> "It's my birthday. I was born on the 53rd of November."

Billy Paultz:

> "I don't believe 60 per cent of what I read on the front page of the newspaper, so why should I believe anything I read on the sports pages?"

CHAPTER 10

BASKETBALL COACHES

"The only thing he guarded was the floor."

Bill Sharman was recognized as an innovator when he coached the Los Angeles Lakers in the mid-1960s. For example, Sharman was one of the first coaches to use game films, a practice which is common in all sports today.

But when Sharman first introduced game films as a coaching tool, he discovered a serious problem. The players would doze off in the darkness. That problem was soon eliminated by another equally-innovative idea.

"We discovered quickly how to keep the players' attention," explained Sharman. "We simply spliced some shots of Playboy bunnies into the game films. We got much better results after that."

John Hopkins University coach **Jim Amen:**

"I've finally got a system whereby we might win some games against Division I schools. Every time we get the ball on offence, we get to ask a player on the opposing team a question in math or science. If the answer is incorrect, we get two points. With some of our opponents, we would probably win by 20."

Denver Nuggets coach **Doug Moe,** *explaining why he doesn't like to be called Mr. Moe:*

"Hey, I don't want to be 'Mister' yet. My body is aging fast but I'm staying immature enough to keep my mentality at a low level."

Cleveland Cavaliers coach **Tom Nissalke:**

"Things are really looking up for us now. For example, general managers around the league are actually going out for lunch now. It used to be they were afraid to go to lunch because they might have missed a phone call from Cleveland offering a trade."

North Carolina State coach **Jim Valvano,** *on the problems of state-rival North Carolina:*

"They've really got some bad problems. They've just lost their senior manager and now they have a new guy slicing the oranges."

Utah Jazz coach **Frank Layden:**

"A good point guard and a good scorer should go hand in hand but not in the locker room."

San Antonio Spurs coach **Cotton Fitzsimmons,** *during a dismal season:*

"Things are so bad I'm getting booed at the supermarket."

Georgia State coach **Roger Couch,** *after his team lost to North Carolina by 44 points:*

"We got beat by one bad call — the one our athletic director made to arrange the game.

Dallas Mavericks coach **Bob Weiss,** *talking about the scoring exploits of one of his players:*

"He's finally doing what I told him. I said: 'Be great' and he has."

University of Rochester coach **Mike Neer,** *after a loss to North Carolina:*

"How can we expect to win the game when three of our starters wanted Phil Ford's autograph?"

DePaul University coach **Ray Meyer,** *after he ordered extra running drills for any players who missed free throws:*

"Either we're going to have the greatest free-throw shooters in the country or the greatest track team."

San Diego State coach **Dave Gaines,** *on the differences between San Diego and the University of Detroit:*

> "At Detroit, we gave the kids room, board and a shotgun. Here, we give them room, board and a surfboard."

University of Texas coach **Abe Lemons,** *after he was fired:*

> "I wish all my friends good luck. But to all those others, and they know who they are, all I can say is that I hope they notice the mistletoe tied to my coat-tails as I leave town."

University of Indiana coach **Bobby Knight:**

> "The ideal coaching job would be at Indiana State prison and there are three reasons for that. First, there is home-court advantage. Secondly, the players' parents won't bother you. And third, there is never any trouble with the alumni."

University of Georgia coach **Hugh Durham,** *on the 45-second shot clock*:

> "That won't be a factor for us. We'll either shoot the ball or throw it away by then."

Frank Layden, *on his first coaching job at St. Agnes High School on Long Island:*

> "I was the JV (junior varsity) coach, the JV baseball coach, the JV football coach, taught five history classes a day, one remedial math class, had bus duty and on Tuesday nights I called bingo numbers. After the first year, the Mother Superior called me in and said I'd done such a good job they were considering making me full-time."

Jim Valvano, *on the differences between North Carolina and his home town of New York:*

> "If you break your watch in North Carolina and ask someone the time, they say: 'Oh, your watch is broken. That's too bad. Come on over to my house.' Then they take you in, make you something to eat and send your watch out to be fixed. In New York, you ask someone the time and they say: 'Whudda I look like, Big Ben?'"

Texas A&M coach **Shelby Metcalf,** *on the shot-blocking ability of an opponent:*

> "You go into the paint against him and he messes up your digestive tract. You'll pass leather for two days."

123

North Texas State coach **Bill Blakeley,** *on his problems with the media:*

"My exact quote was 'suck-egg mule' but it came out 'egg-sucking mule' so you can see some of the problems I'm up against."

Washington State coach **George Raveling,** *on how he got started in basketball:*

"When I went to school in Philadelphia, we only had one coach for both football and basketball. He took all of us who turned out and had us run through a forest. The ones who ran into the trees went on the football team."

Vince Tralka, *the coach of a high school girls' basketball team:*

"We play man-to-man defence, person-to-person sounds like a phone call."

Nevada-Reno coach **Jack Spencer,** *on the defensive weakness of his leading scorer:*

"He's the only player in college basketball who can keep both teams in the game at the same time."

Texas Christian University coach **Jim Killingsworth,** *on the speed of one of his players:*

"He's the only guy I know who's quick enough to play tennis by himself."

Lancaster Lightning coach **Cazzie Russell,** *a former NBA star, trying to explain his emphasis on defence:*

"Hey, just because I didn't play a lot of it myself doesn't mean I can't coach it."

Jacksonville University coach **Bob Wenzel,** *when his team was averaging 25 fouls a game.*

"We're playing that Bell Telephone defence — reach out and touch someone."

Michael Jordan, *comparing coach Dean Smith, for whom he played at North Carolina, and Bobby Knight, for whom he played at the Los Angeles Olympics:*

"They're about the same except for the language."

University of Pittsburgh coach **Roy Chipman,** *about a player who often passed up easy shots:*

> "Sometimes we have to remind him that you don't get any extra points for degree of difficulty."

Abe Lemons:

> "I should have been a track coach. All a track coach has to tell a kid is: 'Keep to your left and get back as soon as you can.' "

Dick Motta, *talking about his home town:*

> "It was so small we didn't even have a village idiot. My brother and I had to take turns."

Ohio Northern coach **Gayle Lauth,** *after one of her players broke a long scoring slump by sinking an 80-foot shot to send the game into overtime:*

> "Well, it's obvious we've been having her shoot from too close to the basket."

Old Dominion coach **Paul Webb,** *after his 500th career win:*

> "Some would say 500 victories is a measure of endurance. Some would say it's a measure of insanity. Depending on the day, I would agree with both."

University of Michigan coach **Bill Frieder,** *on a vacant coaching position:*

> "They should give the job to my wife. She has all the answers."

Utah Jazz coach **Frank Layden,** *about his team's playoff chances:*

> "I'm from Brooklyn. I rooted for the Dodgers. I believe in miracles."

Oklahoma coach **Dave Bliss,** *on his team's offensive problems:*

> "The football team outscores us."

Former Marquette coach **Al McGuire:**

> "If you're gonna love me, you're gonna love me with my curlers."

Jim Valvano, *on the distance of the three-point line:*

"I'm not saying the circle is too close but at halftime my mother came out of the stands and hit three of four."

Houston Rockets coach **Bill Fitch:**

"This year I'm installing three offences, entitled GMA, KISS and SOB. GMA is General Milling Around, KISS is Keep it Simple Stupid and SOB is Save Old Bill."

San Francisco State coach **Lyle Damon,** *when informed his opponents were shooting just 58-per cent from the free-throw line:*

"We defend very well against the free throw."

New York Knicks coach **Hubie Brown,** *walking a player through a defensive manoeuver at practice:*

"Get that forearm up and on me. This ain't college. This is a mugger's league."

Canadian national coach **Jack Donohue:**

"Everyone knows the word 'media' is the plural of 'mediocre.' "

Abe Lemons, *on a colleague known for his flashy wardrobe:*

"His clothes are so loud they set off the airport metal detectors."

San Diego Clippers coach **Jim Lynam,** *after an interviewer suggested he give more than one-word answers:*

"Why?"

Texas A&M coach **Shelby Metcalf,** *on the luck of Houston coach Guy Lewis:*

"He's so lucky. He calls me on the phone and flips a coin for match-ups and darn if he doesn't win every time."

Utah Jazz coach **Frank Layden:**

"Opponents are like your mother-in-law. You're always worried about them and they seem meaner than they really are."

Memphis State coach **Dana Kirk,** *on why most of his players are local boys:*

> "If I have to use more than a tank of gas to recruit, I don't go."

Rod Tueller, *on his move from a local high school to Utah State:*

> "I moved from high school coaching to college coaching without ever moving out of my house. That's unusual. Most of my contemporaries live in mobile homes with the motors running."

Sportswriter **Joe Hamelin,** *about Bobby Knight:*

> "He has a John McEnroe disposition and a Harold Robbins vocabulary and he brings each to his job with the bearing of Patton."

Bradley coach **Dick Versace,** *on how he hires assistant coaches:*

> "I learned a long time ago to hire one with three kids. He'll be in his office working at 8 every morning so he doesn't have to deal with getting the kids off to school."

Abe Lemons, *after he was fired as University of Texas coach:*

> "What am I going to do with all these orange clothes I bought?"

University of Southern California coach **Bonnie Parkhouse,** *on the advantages women athletes have:*

> "There are things you learn on a basketball court you apply in business without even realizing it. Women must learn the ropes — which to climb, which to jump, which to skip. And we're going to have to start playing a little more offence."

Kansas City Kings coach **Cotton Fitzsimmons:**

> "I'd rather coach a team like the Lakers or 76ers and smile 60 nights a year. But you have to play the hand dealt to you."

Missouri coach **Norm Stewart,** *explaining why a top shooter was credited with very few assists:*

> "He doesn't have to pass. You don't want Bob Feller to throw curve balls."

University of Oklahoma coach **Billy Tubbs:**

"I hear Playboy magazine picked us to finish eighth. I didn't see it — I didn't get past the centrefold."

Frank Layden, *comparing himself to Los Angeles Lakers coach Pat Riley:*

"We're both Irish, we're both from New York and we're both good looking. The only difference is that he has his clothes tailored and I find mine."

Stetson University coach **Glenn Wilkes,** *on the dismal fortunes of his team:*

"We don't have a fight song, we have a surrender song."

Jacksonville coach **Bob Wenzel,** *on the number of speaking appearances he's had recently:*

"I've had more engagements than Mickey Rooney."

Paul Westphal, *talking about Tommy Heinsohn, his former coach with the Boston Celtics:*

"I'll always remember his pep talks. One time there were 72 bleeps and that was on Christmas Day."

University of Iowa coach **George Raveling,** *on why he decided to work with the U.S. Olympic basketball team:*

"It's a chance to do something for your country without killing anyone."

Abe Lemons, *denying rumors that he would get the coaching job at Oral Roberts University:*

"I don't think Oral would want me. I smoke and I ain't gonna give up cigars just to coach."

Fordham coach **Tom Penders,** *talking about a 5'9" forward:*

"He's our power forward. We recruited him at Aqueduct Racetrack."

Jim Valvano, *on bedchecks:*

"Last night I made the first bedchecks I've made in 16 years and all the beds were there."

Dallas Mavericks coach **Dick Motta,** *when asked his goal in life:*

> "If I'm one game over .500 when they put me in the box, I'll be happy."

Bobby Knight:

> "I try to learn something from everybody — except the press."

Ohio State coach **Eldon Miller,** *when asked to comment on a published report:*

> "I don't put any credibility in published reports. Heck, I don't even believe my own quotes."

New York Knicks coach **Hubie Brown,** *talking about Moses Malone:*

> "They should give Moses the MVP Trophy and tell him to give it back when he feels like it."

University of Arkansas coach **Doug Barnes,** *when asked what his best decision was this year:*

> "To sell nachos at the concession stands. We're making a bundle off those things."

University of Cincinnati coach **Ed Badger,** *explaining why he often throws his coat to protest officials' calls:*

> "I throw it so the label shows and the crowd can see it. My tailor likes that."

Frank Layden, *after a terrible season:*

> "We had a booster club in Utah this year. By the end of the season it was a terrorist group."

Butler coach **Joe Sexson,** *comparing his team to Kentucky:*

> "Kentucky players put their pants on the same way we do. It just takes them a little longer to pull them up."

Seattle SuperSonics coach **Lenny Wilkens,** *after trading one of his players:*

> "I didn't lose patience with him, I ran out of it."

Abe Lemons, *when asked if he felt bitter about being fired:*

"Not at all, although I plan to buy a glass-bottomed car so I can watch the look on the athletic director's face when I run over him."

Jim Valvano, *on how much he loves to public speak:*

"When I go home and open the refrigerator and the light goes on, I do 20 minutes."

San Diego Clippers assistant coach **Pete Babcock,** *when asked to assess the talent of a draft pick:*

"You asked if he can play for the Clippers and you asked if he can play in the NBA. That's two different questions."

Texas Christian University coach **Jim Killingsworth,** *when asked how his players reacted to being suspended:*

"I don't know. Their stereos were so loud I couldn't tell."

Abe Lemons, *trying to console a player who had scored just one point in a game:*

"You did just great. You scored one more point than a dead man."

Marquette assistant coach **Rick Majerus,** *when asked to take part in a 'roast' for DePaul coach Ray Meyer:*

"Going to Chicago to roast Ray Meyer is like going to India to roast Mother Teresa."

Frank Layden, *on what he might do after retirement:*

"Well, with the death of Orson Welles, Hollywood has an opening for a 300-pound actor."

Iowa State coach **Johnny Orr:**

"When I have something to say, all my players stop to listen. Problem is, I don't usually have anything to say."

George Raveling:

"I understand the TV show 'That's Incredible' has been filming on the Southern California campus. They shot 6 basketball players attending class at the same time."

Billy Tubbs, *after an opposing player blocked four of his team's shots:*

> "I'm going to have to take a few of my guys down to the hospital and have 'Spalding 100' removed from their foreheads."

Washington State coach **Guy Williams,** *talking about a player who does not like to pass the ball:*

> "He had a great average in this game, 18 for 19. He had the ball 19 times and shot it 18."

Vanderbilt coach **C.M. Newton,** *explaining why he always sits near the back of the team plane on charter flights:*

> "I've never heard of a plane that backed into a mountain."

Jim Valvano, *on food prices in Alaska where his team was competing in a tournament:*

> "They had a $100-a-plate dinner for Ronald Reagan while we were there. We made it our pre-game meal. It was just as cheap as ordering off the menu."

Chicago State coach **Bob Hallberg,** *on the team's extensive road schedule:*

> "I think the only person who has liked our schedule so far is my son. He gets the car whenever I'm out of town."

University of Michigan coach **Bill Frieder,** *after the rooms of five of his players were hit by burglars during a road trip:*

> "It's too bad we didn't use our regular airline. That way, our luggage wouldn't have been there."

Oklahoma City coach **Lonnie Nichols,** *on the plight of a coach's wife:*

> "Bless my wife's heart. She grew up as an only child and she thinks she still is."

Kansas City Kings coach **Cotton Fitzsimmons,** *complaining about the lack of respect his team gets on the road:*

> "Whenever we go somewhere to play, it's always ball night, wrist-band night, stocking cap night or something to get somebody in the place."

Missouri coach **Norm Stewart,** *on his team's 80-per cent accuracy from the free-throw line:*

> "We've got a book coming out on that. It's all in the angle of the big toe. We've got a complete explanation — just send us $3.95."

Frank Layden, *after he hired Scott Layden as an assistant:*

> "I didn't hire him because he's my son. I hired him because I'm married to his mother."

University of Richmond coach **Lou Goetz,** *after he married the daughter of former All-American basketball player and major league baseball star Dick Groat:*

> "I married her for her genes. I'm recruiting long range."

Former Marquette coach **Al McGuire,** *talking about the tough neighborhood in which he grew up:*

> "My calling card was a brick."

Former Ohio State coach **Fred Taylor,** *about one of his alumni, Bobby Knight:*

> "He teaches defence a heck of a lot better than he played it. The only thing he guarded in college was the floor."

Former Houston Rockets coach **Tex Winter:**

> "I spent five years of my life coaching two seasons in the NBA."

Duke University coach **Bill Foster,** *when asked to assess his team's chances in an upcoming season:*

> "We won't be spending much time in practice cutting down the nets."

Kentucky coach **Joe B. Hall:**

> "Somebody once said basketball is not a matter of life and death. That's true. At Kentucky, it's more than that."

Denver Nuggets coach **Doug Moe,** *after his team averaged 126.5 points a game while giving up an average of 126.*

> "People keep saying we are the worst defensive team in the league. Actually, we are second — our opponents are worst."

132

Oklahoma coach **Abe Lemons,** *explaining why his players wore a red shoe on one foot and a blue shoe on the other:*

"We wanted to be first in something."

Boston Celtics coach **Bill Fitch,** *to his team at the start of training camp:*

"There are 2,000 sweat glands in the human body. My job is to make sure you use every one of them."

Frank Layden, *on the basic problem facing most coaches:*

"If you gave Michelangelo bad marble, he couldn't make a good statue. You've got to have good material."

CHAPTER 11

GOLFERS

"My best wood today was the pencil."

Deservedly so or not, golf great **Tommy Bolt** had a terrible reputation for temper. They say it was not unusual for Tommy to toss clubs in anger all over the course.

In one tournament, so the story goes, Bolt was 125 yards from the green and asked his caddy for some advice on club selection. The caddy insisted he use a two-iron.

"A two-iron?" cried Bolt. "Are you kidding, I'm only 125 yards away."

"But Tommy," the caddy shot back. "It's the only club left in your bag."

Jack Nicklaus, *on why he still changes his swing after so many successful years:*

"I'm no longer 25 and I can't drive the ball 400 yards any more. You have to change as you go through life. Heck, I even have to change the answers I give my wife."

Arnold Palmer:

"I use a different putting stroke on every hole. I'm not going to let anyone find out my secret."

Lee Trevino, *on the tee of a 600-yard hole:*

"The only way I could get home in two is if I owned a condominium beside the fairway."

Tom Watson, *explaining why he was a poor high school baseball player:*

"I could only hit balls thrown down at my feet."

George Archer:

> "If it weren't for golf, I'd likely be a caddy today."

Radio personality **Al Boliska:**

> "Have you ever noticed what 'golf' spells backward?"

Mark Twain:

> "It's good sportsmanship to not pick up lost golf balls while they are still rolling."

Lee Trevino, *on how fame can be so fleeting:*

> "A woman had me autograph a $5 bill and she told me she would cherish it the rest of her life. A half-hour later I bought some drinks with a $20 bill and got the same $5 bill back in the change."

Sam Snead:

> "The only reason I ever played golf in the first place was so I could afford to hunt and fish."

Arnold Daly:

> "Golf is like a love affair. If you don't take it seriously, it's no fun. If you do take it seriously, it breaks your heart."

Tommy Armour:

> "Golf is an awkward set of bodily contortions designed to produce a graceful result."

Comedian **Joe E. Lewis:**

> "I play in the low 80s. If it's any hotter than that, I won't play."

Lee Trevino, *after a spectator kept 'ooohing and aaahing' about his shots:*

> "Heck, lady, what do you expect from the U.S. Open champion, ground balls?"

Bob Hope:

> "If you watch a game, it's fun. If you play it, it's recreation. If you work at it, it's golf."

136

Chi Chi Rodriguez, *on Jack Nicklaus:*

"Jack has become a legend in his spare time."

Amy Alcott, *describing a key three-wood shot which allowed her to win a tournament:*

"I hit it with everything I've got — 36 C."

Hubert Green:

"Ninety-five per cent of all putts you leave short don't go in."

Lee Trevino, *about his bad back:*

"If it's heavier than a 12-ounce can of beer, I won't pick it up."

Anonymous:

"Golf was once a game for the rich. Now it has millions of poor players."

PGA official **Labron Harris,** *on the rescheduling of the Bob Hope Desert Classic:*

"We think it has a much better chance to be as good as always."

Grier Jones, *when asked what he says to Jack Nicklaus when the two are playing partners:*

"Nice shot, nice shot, nice shot, nice shot, nice shot....."

Lee Trevino, *after he won three tournaments in five weeks:*

"If I keep going like this, I can stop being Mexican and can afford to be a Spaniard."

Mike Morley, *talking about golf in his home state:*

"I played as much golf as I could in North Dakota but the summer up there is pretty short. It was usually on a Tuesday."

Dave Stockton, *after Al Geiberger fired an amazing 13-under-par 59 in the Memphis Classic:*

"This was the greatest round of golf ever played and I had the honor of keeping Al's card. I ought to win the low score-keeping award."

Ray Floyd, *after he put nine straight 3s on his scorecard:*
"I like 3s. They're easier to add up."

Chi Chi Rodriguez, *after a bad round:*
"The best wood in my bag today was the pencil."

Lee Trevino, *on his divorce:*
"It was a friendly divorce. She left me the piano and the lawnmower. I couldn't play either one."

Seve Ballesteros, *when asked if he had one special girlfriend:*
"No, that would be like playing the same course all the time."

Jim Nelford, *explaining why he plays right-handed but putts left-handed:*
"My father was left-handed and my mother was right-handed. When I was growing up, I used whatever clubs I could get."

Bob Hope:
"Golf is the best tension reliever in the world. It's a great game for guys who are too old for girls but who still want to get into a trap."

Frustrated golfer:
"This is a terrible game. I'm glad I don't have to play again until tomorrow."

Lee Trevino, *who always enjoyed the Florida portion of the PGA Tour more than any other:*
"You know what the abbreviation for California stands for, don't you? Come And Live In Florida."

Anonymous:
"Life is like golf. You spend years trying to reach the green and you still end up in the hole."

Jack Nicklaus:
"If you're a good putter, you're a good putter."

Anonymous:

> "I hope I don't live long enough for them to develop a machine that will enable me to look at an instant replay of my game."

Hugh Allen:

> "What this country needs is a pill that can make a man enjoy raking leaves more than playing golf."

Gary Player, *explaining his decision to return to the PGA Tour:*

> "I have six kids and 107 quarterhorses to feed and I'm not sure which group eats more."

Golfer, to his playing partner:

> "You've got a real picture-book swing. Too bad a few pages are missing."

Lee Trevino:

> "Your name is written on a tournament before you even tee it up."

Laura Baugh, *after giving birth to her first child:*

> "If you can cope with the anxiety of being pregnant and giving birth, you can definitely handle the rigors of golf."

Fuzzy Zoeller, *right after he missed the cut, to a fan who had asked if he had a minute to sign an autograph:*

> "A minute? I've got the whole darn weekend."

JoAnne Carner, *talking about the suggestive poses of Jan Stephenson in 'Fairway' magazine:*

> "If I had legs like that, I'd pose that way too. Don't they have a 'Miss Piggy' category?"

Eddy Coates, *an employee at the British Embassy in Beirut, on the difficulties of playing golf with planes, gunners and anti-aircraft weapons blazing away in the battle-torn city:*

> "It destroys your putting."

Lee Trevino, *on the rough at the British Open:*

> "At No. 15, we put down my bag to hunt for a ball. Found the ball, lost the bag."

Amateur **Jim Holtgrieve,** *when asked what was the highlight of his two-under-par 70 in the first round of the Masters:*

"Playing with Arnold Palmer."

Bob Hope, *after receiving the first male membership ever offered by the Ladies Professional Golf Association:*

"Does this mean I get to drive from the women's tees?"

Chi Chi Rodriguez, *after he hit into the water on two consecutive holes:*

"I must have thought I was Jacques Cousteau."

Bill Rogers, *after winning 19-million yen ($65,000 US) in a Japanese tournament:*

"I finally did it. I became a yenionaire."

Golf legend **Bobby Jones,** *about Jack Nicklaus:*

"The other players in this tournament were here to play golf. Jack plays a game with which I am not familiar."

Lee Trevino:

"If the money's there, I'll play on a gravel road."

Tom Watson, *after being slapped with a two-stroke penalty for breaking a rule:*

"There is no surer nor more painful way to learn a rule than to be penalized once for breaking it."

Anonymous pro golfer:

"Second place in a tournament is like eating day-old donuts. The dough isn't bad but it isn't satisfying either."

Writer **Herbert Warren Wind:**

"Golf is unique among action sports in that a man can be lacking in youth, brawn, speed of foot, suppleness of muscle, clearness of eye and other athletic virtues and still be a pretty fair golfer."

Lee Trevino, *after losing to Johnny Miller in the Tuscon Open, the first tournament of the season:*

"The Mormons have it all over us early in the year. Most of us haven't had a chance to dry out from the winter."

LEE TREVINO: "MY WIFE TELLS ME SHE DOESN'T CARE WHAT I DO WHEN I'M AWAY, AS LONG AS I'M NOT ENJOYING IT."

Anonymous caddy, about golfers on the PGA Tour:
> "They treat us like divots."

Jack Nicklaus, *on putting:*
> "Aim it and knock it in."

Dentist, as his golf ball rolled toward the cup:
> "Open wider, please."

Dick Grimm *of the Royal Canadian Golf Association, after watching Greg Norman tee off:*
> "If I took a swing at the ball the way he does, I'd be in traction until Christmas."

Patty Sheehan, *on why she turned pro:*
> "It wasn't much fun being an amateur. I got tired of polishing the silverware."

Bruce Lietzke, *to everyone within earshot when Lee Trevino walked onto the practice tee:*
> "There goes the neighborhood."

Bob Hope:
> "I swim several times a day. It's easier than buying new golf balls."

Kansas City Royals third baseman **George Brett,** *talking about one of his golf games:*
> "I was three over — one over the house, one over the patio and one over the swimming pool."

Amateur golfer **Elaine Johnson,** *after her tee shot sliced off a tree, bounced back at her and dropped into her bra:*
> "I don't mind taking a stroke penalty but I'll be darned if I'm going to play it where it lies."

Anonymous golfer:
> "The frustration of golf is in the disparity between what you should have done and what you actually did."

Lee Trevino:

"My caddy is so fat, I just look to see where he's standing and then I know the putt breaks that way."

Caddy, to a golfer who was having such a bad game that he threatened to drown himself in the lake:

"You won't drown. You can't keep your head down."

Golf fan **Judith Dunkle,** *describing the ideal spectator:*

"The perfect spectator must have the eye of an eagle, the neck of a giraffe, the skin of an alligator and the bladder of an elephant."

Anonymous golf pro:

"Our course has 20 holes. It's cheaper than filling those two potholes in the parking lot."

Lee Trevino:

"The only time I stop talking is when I'm asleep."

Anonymous golfer, after his playing partner, a judge, won the previous hole:

"Your honor, your honor."

Sam Snead, *on the frustrations of golf:*

"If a man comes home with sand in his cuffs and cockleburs in his pants, don't ask him what he shot."

University of Southern California freshman **Mike Blewett,** *after a hole-in-one:*

"When I saw the ball bounce into the cup, I didn't know how to react. All I could think of was: 'Good, I don't have to putt.' "

Anonymous:

"Sinking a 30-foot putt to save triple-bogey is like putting whip cream on horse manure."

Jan Stephenson, *after she received a telephone bill for $136,000:*

"Someone got my credit card number. I think it must have been some terrorists. You can't believe some of the countries they called — countries I never heard of."

Lee Trevino, *on how to avoid being hit by lightning:*

"Walk to the clubhouse holding a one-iron over your head. Not even the good Lord can hit a one-iron."

Mark Twain:

"Golf is a good walk spoiled."

Jack Nicklaus, *when asked how many MacGregor golf gloves he uses in a day:*

"I used to use three a round but since I bought the company I use only one."

Hale Irwin, *about the accuracy of sports writers:*

"I don't drink coffee. It bothers me when a reporter writes that we sat down and talked over a cup of coffee. It may add atmosphere but it's simply not true."

Anonymous Chicago Bears fan:

"My golf game has suffered ever since I started using Chicago Bears golf balls — two yards to the left, three yards to the right."

Lee Trevino, *on golf:*

"The good Lord never gives you everything at the same time. If your drives are on, your short game is off and if your putter is hot, your fairway irons are cold. It's like having a 38-inch bust, you also get fat legs."

Chi Chi Rodriguez, *when asked what his caddy told him before a crucial putt:*

"He told me to keep the ball low."

PGA commissioner **Deane Beman,** *on the integrity of golf:*

"Golf may be the only sport left that still observes those ideals of conduct and integrity. There are no spitballs in golf."

George Archer, *about Lee Trevino:*

"The only time he's off the fairway is when he's answering the phone."

Tommy Bolt, *when asked who was the greatest golfer of all time:*

> "All I know is that Jack Nicklaus watches Ben Hogan practise and I never heard of Hogan watching Nicklaus."

Lee Trevino, *on being hit by lightning at the 1975 Western Open:*

> "My whole life flashed in front of me and I couldn't believe I was that bad."

Ben Crenshaw, *about Tom Watson's chip shot at the 17th hole which assured him of victory in the U.S. Open:*

> "They should erect a plaque on that spot. I could stand there and hit 500 balls without doing that."

Harry Crosby, *on his father Bing:*

> "Dad always said if you want to find out all about a person, as a business partner or a son-in-law, just play a round of golf with him."

Sam Snead, *on why golf is more challenging than baseball:*

> "In golf, when we hit a foul ball, we've got to go out and play it."

Lee Trevino, *explaining the advice he got from his doctor about his bad back:*

> "He told me not to practise so much. He said that after 32 years I ought to know how to play by now. So now I only hit a bucket of balls each day. Besides, it gives me more time to drink beer."

Al Geiberger, *after he shot a 13-under-par 59 in the Memphis Classic:*

> "They'll remember me for this."

Ray Floyd, *when asked if he could duplicate his great round the next day:*

> "I see no reason why my game should go sour while I'm asleep."

Bob Hope:

> "I'm going to shoot my age some day, even if I have to live to be 115 to do it."

Abe Lemons, *basketball coach at the University of Texas, about his play in a coaches' golf tournament:*

"I wasn't pleased. I hit my longest drive 250 yards but the trouble was it came on a 175-yard hole."

Cathy Sherk, *commenting on her rookie year on the LPGA tour:*

"I'm proud of the fact that I only hit one ball out of bounds all year. On that one, I was right in the middle of my backswing when my bra strap broke. I didn't mind that so much but I had a heck of a time teeing up the next one."

Doug Sanders, *who developed a reputation as a late-night party person while on the PGA Tour:*

"I give a guy in Los Angeles $50 an hour just to sleep for me."

Lee Trevino:

"There are two things that cannot win — dogs that chase cars and golfers who miss greens."

Lance Ten Broeck, *on why he keeps trying to qualify for the PGA Tour:*

"I'm broke and I don't want to get a real job. All I own are a Porsche and a suntan."

Lee Trevino:

"My swing's not much but it's good for a short fat man."

Tom Watson, *after hearing a complaint that most pro golfers lacked personality:*

"The personality of golf is good golf. If you want a comedian, tune in 'Saturday Night Live.' "

Fuzzy Zoeller, *following his win in the Masters:*

"I was so nervous Saturday night, I went to bed at 10 p.m. and got up at 10:15."

JoAnne Carner, *after her 30th career victory:*

"You need 30 wins to qualify for the Hall of Fame. It's important to me. Besides it makes a good obituary."

Golf fan:

"I don't know how Bruce Lietzke can hit the ball that far. I tee up the ball the exact same way he does."

CHAPTER 12

TENNIS PLAYERS

"Their rivalry is narrower than my girlfriend's mind."

As the commercial says, some people like John McEnroe and some people, well, let's just say they are undecided.

In Little Rock, Ark., one subdivision has streets with tennis names such as Wimbledon Loop and Davis Cup Lane. The residents of that neighborhood once asked city officials to name another street McEnroe Court. That request was turned down.

"Are we talking about the guy who is always complaining?" asked board member **Gale Weeks**. "I don't think we should name anything in this city after him. I would agree to anyone else but he's a spoiled brat."

Bill Cosby, *on tennis:*

"Footwork is very important. If you try to move without picking up your legs, the feet get very angry and start to step on one another."

Martina Navratilova:

"In Czechoslovakia, there is no such thing as freedom of the press. In the United States, there is no such thing as freedom from the press."

Tennis great **Helen Wills Moody:**

"If you see a tennis player who looks as if he is working hard, then that means he isn't very good."

John McEnroe, *after he prevented Jimmy Connors from winning a tournament for the sixth time:*

"Jimmy has won it enough."

Pam Shriver, *after she was described in a national magazine as 'positively stunning':*

"I was amazed it took someone that long to write it."

Ilie Nastase, *when asked if he ever had second thoughts about his behavior on the court:*

"No. Why should I? The crowd doesn't have second thoughts for me. And when I lose, they're happy."

Guillermo Vilas, *after playing in 95-degree weather in Washington, D.C.:*

"I think they should speak with the mayor here to put some air conditioning on his courts."

Anonymous:

"Don't get romantically involved with a tennis player, because to them love means nothing."

Billie Jean King, *nearing the end of her competitive career:*

"I'm simply no longer willing to pay the price of everyday workouts."

Australian tennis player **John McCurdy:**

"My favorite shot is the short smash while my opponent is lying on the ground."

Roscoe Tanner, *after losing to John McEnroe 6-1, 6-2:*

"I only made one mistake today. I got up."

Chris Evert, *joking after losing another match to Martina Navratilova:*

"Why don't you go join the men's tour and leave us alone?"

Ilie Nastase:

"I have this dream in which I win Wimbledon. Then I take my trophy and I go all around that crazy stadium bowing to the people and giving the finger to everybody. Then I take my racquets and break them up with my hands. Then I throw them in the river and stop playing tennis."

John McEnroe, *after a lady yelled an obscenity at him during an exhibition match in Miami:*

> "Thanks lady, you just gave me a good line for the U.S. Open."

Arthur Ashe, *describing Martina Navratilova:*

> "She's like the old Green Bay Packers. You know exactly what she's going to do but there isn't a thing you can do about it."

South African **Ray Moore,** *explaining how to beat Bjorn Borg:*

> "All you have to do is get to the net and make the shot of your life every time."

Chris Evert:

> "Anyone who is aggressive, who can serve and volley and who can keep the ball in play gives me trouble. The others I can usually handle well."

Bill Cosby's *advice to beginners:*

> "Work on your footwork and buy intelligent balls."

Martina Navratilova, *describing her doubles partnership with Pam Shriver:*

> "You can't go through us and you can't go over us. What do you do? I wouldn't want to play us, that's for sure."

Jimmy Connors, *on his reputation as a brat:*

> "I guess people thought I was a brat because they had never seen anything like me before. Maybe they never will again, at least until my son comes along."

Billie Jean King:

> "I've seldom played well when I haven't felt mentally tough but I would never deliberately concede anything to anyone."

John McEnroe, *when asked by a reporter what the media should say to fans who don't understand him:*

> "Let me give it some thought. I'll get back to you in a couple of years."

Arthur Ashe, *on his retirement:*

"I am ending my non-stop odyssey in search of the perfect serve."

Wendy Turnbull, *on her social life:*

"I know nuns with better social lives than me."

Ilie Nastase, *on the trouble caused by his quick temper and his gesturing to the crowd:*

"If you could have amputated my middle finger years ago, I'd have about $2 million more in the bank today."

Tennis analyst **Bud Collins:**

"The rivalry between Chris Evert-Lloyd and Martina Navratilova is extraordinary and the margin betwen the two is narrower than my girlfriend's mind."

CHAPTER 13

BOXERS

"I tried to stay busy on him."

George Chuvalo was a great Canadian heavyweight champion. In 97 professional fights, he was never knocked off his feet, despite facing the likes of Muhammad Ali, Joe Frazier, Floyd Patterson and George Foreman.

After he hung up the gloves, Chuvalo was asked to compare himself to new Canadian champion Trevor Berbick.

"I could beat Berbick six weeks after I'm dead."

Muhammad Ali, *as he refused induction into the U.S. Army:*

"I ain't got no quarrel with them Viet Congs."

Randall 'Tex' Cobb, *after a lop-sided loss to heavyweight champion Larry Holmes:*

"The next time I might move my head. I know it sounds crazy but I've seen other people do it and it seems to work."

Referee **Lucien Joubert,** *after he received only $950 for working the heavyweight title fight between Muhammad Ali and Leon Spinks:*

"It was such an historic event I would have done it for nothing."

Sports reporter, to 36-year-old **George Jerome** *prior to his fight with 41-year-old George Chuvalo:*

"Will your youth be an advantage?"

Sugar Ray Leonard:

"We all have God-given talents. Mine just happens to be beating up people."

'Two-ton' Tony Galento, *giving the same prediction before every fight:*

"I'll moida da bum."

Rocky Marciano:

"I never liked boxing. I hated the training part and I certainly didn't enjoy hurting people. I don't know what happened to me in the ring. I'd see the films of myself going crazy, swinging both fists, always moving forward and wonder if that was really me. To tell you the truth, I'd much rather have been a big league baseball player. I loved baseball. I used boxing to make money because I was good at it but I never ever liked it."

Muhammad Ali, *before his fight with Larry Holmes:*

"It ain't gonna be no match. I will be supremely superior." (He lost.)

Long-time boxing man **Yancey Durham:**

"Boxing is bad for you. You can get killed."

Leon Spinks, *to police after he was arrested for driving his car through a fence adjacent to a shopping mall:*

"I was looking at the property for a possible training site."

Scranton, Pa., mayor **James McNulty,** *on boxing promoter Don King:*

"I was vice-mayor in 1975 when we gave Don King the key to the city. Since then, I've become mayor and we've changed the locks."

Defeated boxer with a black eye:

"I sort of got what he had coming."

Hilmer Kenty, *describing his stategy in a fight against Ernesto Espana:*

"I tried to stay busy on him."

Sportswriter **Dick Young,** *after Larry Holmes stopped Marvis Frazier in the first round:*

"The most surprising part of the fight was that none of the judges called the round even."

"FLOAT LIKE A BUTTERFLY, STING LIKE A BEE."

Muhammad Ali, *on speculation he might try to regain the championship a fourth time:*

"I will shock the earth again."

Lon Simmons, *on his short-lived career as a professional boxer:*

"I was once offered $300 to throw a fight in the third round but I had to turn it down because I had never made it to the third round."

Sugar Ray Leonard, *about Roberto Duran:*

"If he were my neighbor, I'd move."

Sportswriter **Mark Whicker,** *describing the comeback of Joe Frazier against Jumbo Cummings, both somewhat overweight:*

"It looked like mating season at the walrus cage."

Rocky Graziano, *on fellow-fighter Jake LaMotta:*

"When LaMotta gets dressed up, he looks like a stolen car."

Muhammad Ali, *during the height of his fame:*

"It's funny how a boxer can be better known than a country."

Johnny Carson, *talking about Larry Holmes who received some low blows in a fight with Gerry Cooney:*

"Holmes just signed to sing with the Temptations."

Tex Cobb:

"People always ask me if success is going to change me and I tell them I sure hope so."

Nova Spinks, *estranged wife of Leon Spinks, before his fight with Larry Holmes:*

"I am confident Leon will win and I want to take my confidence in him all the way to the bank."

Frank Sinatra, *following the death of boxing great Joe Louis:*

"The man who never rested on canvas, may he rest lightly on clouds."

Former heavyweight champion **Joe Frazier,** *after losing a few dollars at the blackjack tables in Las Vegas:*

"The next time, I'm going to get all those dealers and put them in the ring with Larry Holmes."

Former boxer **Art Aragon,** *after Roberto Duran quit in the eighth round of his fight with Sugar Ray Leonard:*

"If you're going into the tank, learn how to swim."

Ray 'Boom Boom' Mancini, *after a visit to the White House to meet President Reagan:*

"It's just like meeting Santa Claus. You go in, get your picture taken with him and then leave."

Airline stewardess, to Muhammad Ali after he refused to do up his seat belt by saying: 'Superman don't need no seat belt':

"Superman don't need no airplane either."

Tex Cobb, *commenting on the possibility of another fight with Larry Holmes:*

"I doubt it. I don't think his hands can take the abuse any more."

Muhammad Ali, *explaining the big change in his life after he retired from the ring:*

"It's changed a lot. Johnny Carson doesn't call me any more."

Promoter **Don King:**

"Boxing is a very interesting business. It's predicated on lies."

Roberto Duran, *when asked what position he played as a little league baseball player in Panama:*

"Anywhere I wanted."

Sugar Ray Leonard, *before his bout with Ayub Kalule:*

"I heard Kalule's got a witch doctor. I don't really believe in it but why take chances?"

Joe Frazier, *on the individuality of boxing:*

"You've got to do your own road work. If you don't, no one can help you."

Larry Holmes, *when asked why he wanted $100 million to step back into the ring:*

"Because it's a nice round figure."

Muhammad Ali:

"I was always afraid that the other guy was going to try to hurt me if he could. So I took all my fear and did a little act, saying how confident I was and all that P.R., just to try to use it to deal with the fear the opponent also had to have. If you're not afraid when you step in the ring, you're crazy, and who wants crazy people in boxing?"

Boxing analyst **Dr. Ferdie Pacheco:**

"If Rocky Marciano fought today, there would be no way that he'd be undefeated. He cut like the Panama Canal."

Trevor Berbick:

"I never use my mind very much because I know what psychology is all about."

Bob Hope, *talking about his boxing career:*

"I was pretty good at the YMCA level but then I got in with guys who could hit."

Sportswriter **Mike Lupica,** *describing Livingstone Bramble:*

"Every guy he fights has the home-planet advantage."

Larry Holmes, *on how good a football player he was in his younger days:*

"If I had stuck with it, you never would have heard of O.J. Simpson and Tony Dorsett."

Joe Frazier, *when asked why he still referred to Muhammad Ali as Cassius Clay:*

"Because it makes him mad."

Ray Miller, *a boxer known for his great left hook:*

"When I hit a guy with the hook, if he didn't go down he at least did some funny things with his feet."

Aaron Pryor, *on his public image:*

"I'm not a psycho for real, just in the media."

Keith Strauss, *manager of one-time heavyweight contender Ron Stander, on his man's idea of training:*

"His idea of fight preparation is cutting down from one case of beer a night to three six-packs a night."

Don King, *praising the American judicial system after his acquittal on tax-evasion charges:*

"If I were in the Soviet Union, I'd be a black iceblock in Siberia by now."

Reporter, to a fighter who had two black eyes and a broken cheekbone:

"Did he go for your head at all?"

Muhammad Ali, *about Larry Holmes:*

"Holmes is so ugly that when he was a kid and he started to cry, the tears would stop, go back and then roll down the back of his head."

CHAPTER 14

SOCCER PLAYERS AND OTHER ATHLETES

"It depends on who Jane is."

When it comes to passionate fans, there is none more so than a soccer fan. Take **Trevor George** of Penarth, Wales, for example.

When Trevor and Lynette had a baby girl, proud papa decided to name her after twenty of the world's greatest players. Mr. George registered his daughter's names as — hold your breath — Jennifer, Edson Arantes do Nascimento (Pele), Jairzinho, Rivellino, Carlos-Alberto, Paulo-Cesar, Brietner, Cruyff, Greaves, Charlton, Best, Moore, Ball, Keegan, Banks, Gray, Francis, Brooking, Curtis, Toshack, Law George.

Lynette was so angry she left Trevor and went home to her mother. She also managed to cancel the registration and rename the baby Jennifer Anne George.

Trevor was incensed. "She can stay where she is if that's what she's going to do," he raged. "I'm more angry about her changing the names than I am about her leaving me."

Italian journalist **Giampiero Masieri,** *explaining the importance of soccer in his country:*
"First love, second football. Photo finish maybe."

Mickey Rooney, *on his career at the race track:*
"I lost $5 at Santa Anita 40 years ago and I've spent something like $2 million trying to win it back."

Race car driver **Sam Posey,** *arguing that his sport is the most demanding:*
"You can't throw an incomplete pass here."

Bruce Jenner, *1976 Olympic decathlon champion:*

"I spent 12 years training for a career that was over in one week."

Edson Arantes do Nascimento, *discussing his nickname 'Pele':*

"I don't know what it means but I'm lucky my friends gave it to me as a boy because it's easy for everyone in the world to say."

Marilyn Bell, *after swimming across Lake Ontario in 1954:*

"I did it for Canada."

Track star **Carl Lewis,** *after the world championships in Helsinki:*

"I had problems with a bee at both the start and finish. I hope it wasn't the same one. I'd expect to run faster than a bee."

Race car driver/actor **Paul Newman:**

"I think the greatest honor I've ever had was to be No. 19 on Richard Nixon's enemy list."

New York Arrows soccer goaltender **Zoltan Toth,** *on the dangers of facing the cannon machine in practice:*

"Before I step in, I always have my last cigarette."

Anonymous:

"Skiing is a sport in which you try to avoid the breaks of the game."

Race car driver **Cale Yarborough,** *on his philosophy of life:*

"Never wrestle with a pig — you'll both get dirty but the pig will enjoy it."

Race track saying:

"Never bet against an unbeaten horse."

Soccer player **Gordon Hill,** *after he was traded to his fourth team in less than a year:*

"I've had more homes than Century 21."

Bill Rodgers, *comparing marathon running with football:*

"Passing a football straight is nice and dandy but I think it's an inferior skill. I'll be running over Joe Namath's grave."

Sportscaster **Dick Beddoes:**

"Horses and jockeys mature earlier than people, which is why horses are admitted to race tracks at the age of two and jockeys before they are old enough to shave."

Tony Hulman, *at the Indianapolis 500:*

"Gentlemen, start your engines."

New York Cosmos goaltender **David Brcic:**

"We have a very good team. If this club plays properly all the time, my mother could play goal."

Sportswriter **Jim Cressman,** *on the pressure of figure skating:*

"It's okay to have butterflies in your stomach before a big competition, as long as they fly in formation."

Diane Jones-Konihowski, *at the 1978 Commonwealth Games:*

"This is the biggest moment in my life, besides the time I married a Ukrainian Eskimo."

Sixty-five-year-old **Ashby Harper,***when asked how he felt after swimming the English Channel:*

"Old and cold."

Ray Klivecka, *coach of the Buffalo Stallions of the Major Indoor Soccer League:*

"When you get to be 32 years of age as a soccer player, you push the down button on the elevator and you get off when it stops."

Stock car racer **Buddy Baker,** *talking about all the drivers who change racing teams:*

"Thank goodness for Yankee owner George Steinbrenner. Otherwise, we might be the laughing stock of pro sport."

Angela Kondrak, *after she failed in her attempt to swim across Lake Ontario at the age of 14:*

"Marathon swimming isn't a bed of roses."

Ron Grant, *following his 217-day, 8,574-mile run around Australia:*

"I've always liked to run and I wanted to be the first person to run around Australia. I didn't realize it was so big."

Julio Mazzei, *after being hired as coach for the second time by the New York Cosmos:*

"I'm the Bob Lemon of soccer."

Race driver **Pancho Carter,** *on why he's involved in such a risky business:*

"I'm too lazy to work and too chicken to steal."

Comedian **Bill Cosby,** *on his chances of winning a 400-metre race in the masters division of the Penn Relays:*

"I don't know what will happen. I may pull a groin muscle and go to the wheelchair division."

Vic Spellberg, *trying to describe the sport of powerboat racing:*

"It's like jumping into a cold shower, hitting yourself over the head with a baseball bat and tearing up $100 bills, all at the same time."

San Diego Sockers goaltender **Volkmar Gross,** *when asked what he thinks about when the play is at the other end:*

"Did I pay the phone bill?"

Race car driver **Tom Sneva:**

"Our sport is a lot different from a lot of other sports. For example, a professional basketball player doesn't have to worry about his shoes burning out in the middle of a game."

Carol Lewis, *explaining why she and her brother Carl became great track stars:*

"Our folks used to run us dead and put us to bed."

Mickey Rooney, *on his love for the racetrack:*

"The racetrack is like a second home for me. It used to be my first home too, until I lost it at the windows."

Vancouver Whitecaps spokesman **Jack Leonard,** *commenting on a player who was once fined for 'mooning' the opposition:*

"We bought him a very expensive belt this year."

Hall of Fame trainer **Hirsch Jacobs,** *on the best advice he could give a jockey:*

"Go to the front immediately and turn left as fast as you can."

Distance swimmer **Marilyn Bell,** *to Cindy Nicholas after Cindy swam across Lake Ontario in August, 1974:*

"It's your lake now."

Chris Whitlock *of Washington State, explaining why he was able to post such a fine time in the 400 metres:*

"I looked up and saw this javelin coming."

San Diego Sockers coach **Ron Newman,** *talking about one of his more outspoken players:*

"He can do almost everything with his feet, except keep them out of his mouth."

Dennis Rainear, *after he ran the last 16 miles of the Grand Valley Marathon with a bullet in his head:*

"I regret such a silly thing slowed me down."

Stock car racer **Richard Petty,** *after it was suggested to him that he run for the Republican party in North Carolina:*

"I've never run for second place in my life and I'm not going to start now."

Anonymous downhill skier:

"I can do a dandy slalom, mainly on my spinal column."

Walt Chyzowych, *the coach of the U.S. national team, on why he feels soccer is such a democratic game:*

"For one, anybody can play regardless of size. Secondly, on the field the player is given the freedom to show what he can do and the responsibility to make his own decisions. Once you've got the principles of the game in mind, you're the genius."

Daley Thompson:

"Being a decathlete is like having 10 girlfriends. You have to love them all and you can't afford losing one."

Comedian **Rodney Dangerfield,** *on jogging:*

"The trouble with jogging is that by the time you realize you're in shape for it, it's too far to walk back."

Race driver **Geoff Brabham:**

"Racing is 99 per cent boredom and one per cent terror."

Terry Hanson, *the general manager of the Atlanta Chiefs soccer team, talking about one of his quietest players:*

"The guy is so quiet he mails home blank postcards."

Olympic swimmer **Steve Lundquist,** *when asked if he'd like to play Tarzan in the movies:*

"It depends on who Jane is.

Sam Rubin, *the owner of John Henry who won more than $3 million during his horse-racing career:*

"I'm worried that some day John Henry is going to ask me what I've done with all of his money."

Track star **Willie Gault,** *after becoming the first man to win both the 60-yard dash and the 60-yard high hurdles in the NCAA indoor track and field meet:*

"It's the first time anybody's been dumb enough to try."

Actress **Elizabeth Taylor:**

"I prefer rugby to soccer. When soccer players start biting each other's ears off again, maybe I'll like it better."

The P.A. announcer at Atlanta International Raceway, after Cale Yarborough's wallet was stolen:

"Would the man who has Cale Yarborough's wallet please keep the money and return the personal papers inside? And God help you if Cale ever finds out who you are."

Joseph Moakley, *a Democrat from Massachusetts, talking about marathoner Bill Rodgers:*

"It's good to have a guy running in my district that I don't have to worry about."

Montreal Manic soccer coach **Eddie Firmani,** *talking about the state of the game in his homeland:*

"The population of Italy consists of 60 million soccer coaches."

Richard Petty, *on retirement:*

"No one wants to quit when he's losing and no one wants to quit when he's winning."

CHAPTER 15

SPORTS MEDIA

"You can't lateral a horse."

Howard Cosell and **Al Michaels** were driving back to their Kansas City hotel on June 7, 1981. While the limousine was stopped at a red light in a poor part of the city, Howard noticed two young men fighting. Three other young men were shouting encouragement.

Reluctantly, the driver obeyed orders to pull over to the curb. Cosell got out of the car, stuck a cigar in his mouth, strolled over to the fight and began to, well, be Howard. He critiqued the boxing talents of each fighter (according to Howard neither was very good), jokingly rebuked all five for their behavior and declared the bout finished in typical 'Cosellian' fashion.

For their part, the five young men were in shock. They could not believe this was actually Howard Cosell. They listened, obeyed, shook his hand and then spent several minutes chatting and laughing.

Eventually, Cosell returned to the limousine but not before one of the young men was heard to say that, if it had been anyone else but Howard Cosell, he would have regretted making such an approach.

Michaels, who wisely stayed in the car during the entire episode, recalled it humorously by saying: "I didn't think I was necessarily going to die. I was thinking more in terms of serious injury."

Sportswriter **Red Smith,** *about Howard Cosell:*
"I have tried, honestly tried, to like Howard. I have failed."

New York Yankees broadcaster **Mel Allen,** *about a home run ball:*
"It's going, going, gone."

Scott Ostler:

"The TV coverage of pro football is sadly lacking in one area. They should have remote cameras in the homes of the players' mothers. That way, when sideline cameras zero in on a player saying: 'Hi Mom' the remote cameras could get a shot of the mother mouthing: 'Hi Son.' "

Foster Hewitt:

"Good evening Canada and hockey fans in the United States."

John Madden, *on how a running back learns to avoid tacklers:*

"It's like a rat in an experiment. If he turns left, he gets the cheese. If he turns right, he gets hit on the head with a mallet. It doesn't take long to learn."

Bob Uecker, *talking about his major league baseball career:*

"The more I played, the closer I was to going back to the minors. I tried not to play."

Earl Weaver, *while working as a World Series commentator, on Baltimore Orioles catcher Rick Dempsey:*

"Dempsey's ability will never continue to amaze me."

Bob Costas, *after partner Tony Kubek wondered out loud who invented the 'wave':*

"Claiming credit for inventing the 'wave' is like taking credit for designing the leisure suit."

Curt Gowdy, *talking about the fact that some high draft picks fail while lower picks succeed:*

"You never know. You can't open their heads and look into their hearts."

Joe Garagiola, *after Dave Winfield of the New York Yankees hit a 425-foot, line-drive home run over the centre field fence:*

"If you could slice that hit into singles, you'd have a heckuva season."

Frank Gifford, *describing his longtime role between Howard Cosell and Don Meredith on Monday Night Football telecasts:*

"Sometimes, I felt more like the resident psychiatrist than the play-by-play man."

Atlanta Hawks broadcaster **Skip Caray,** *on Utah Jazz centre Danny Schayes, the son of Hall of Famer Dolph Schayes:*

"He looks a lot like his father but he plays more like his mother."

Detroit Tigers broadcaster **Ernie Harwell:**

"A baseball broadcaster is a guy who can identify a slider at 200 feet but can't tell you the color of his wife's eyes."

Sports journalist **Larry King:**

"Why does the guy who gives tips at the racetrack often need a ride home?"

University of Michigan football coach **Bo Schembechler,** *talking about his son:*

"The poor kid has a warped mind. He wants to be a sportswriter."

Howard Cosell:

"I think I've made a difference in my phase of the broadcast industry but I don't think I've impacted on the world in the manner of Franklin Roosevelt."

Baseball broadcaster **Jerry Coleman:**

"He slides into second with a stand-up double."

John McEnroe, *on reporters:*

"I can't rationalize talking to these people because they're not rational."

Anonymous broadcaster:

"Things are going so badly for some baseball teams that by the fifth inning they start selling hot dogs to go."

TV interviewer **Dave Hodge,** *after Willi Plett of the Minnesota North Stars interrupted the conversation by leaning over and taking a pair of scissors to Hodge's tie:*

"That's great Willi. I didn't know you could cut to your right."

Al McGuire, *on the fact that NBC covered college basketball all season but CBS televised the NCAA finals:*

"It's like getting all the dances with the girl but when it comes time to take her home and get in the rumble seat, CBS is touchin' all the soft spots."

Los Angeles Dodgers broadcaster **Vin Scully,** *about pitcher Burt Hooton:*

"He's such a quiet person that the night the Dodgers won the World Series, he went out and painted the town beige."

Baseball broadcaster **Dizzy Dean,** *after he was criticized for not knowing the King's English:*

"Ol' Diz knows the King's English. Heck, he knows the Queen is English too."

NBC analyst **Pete Axthelm,** *after the network began showing CFL games during the NFL players' strike:*

"The Calgary Stampeders will never be America's team."

Horse race announcer **Clem McCarthy,** *after he made a big mistake during the stretch run of the Preakness:*

"You can't lateral a horse."

Kansas City Royals broadcaster **Fred White,** *when the ticker tape from the out-of-town games mistakenly showed the same starter and reliever for the Minnesota Twins:*

"Well, I see in the game at Minnesota that Terry Felton has relieved himself on the mound in the second inning."

Toronto Blue Jays broadcaster **Early Wynn,** *describing a potential double play:*

"They done do'd it at second but they didn't done do'd it at first."

Joe Kapp, *talking about his qualifications for a football coaching job in California:*

"If Howard Cosell can coach all the pro teams in the world, why can't I coach the Golden Bears?"

170

TALK

TALK

TALK

CHATTER

I LUV NG

ALL THE ANSWERS

SPORT ENCYCLOPEDIA

BOXING FOOTBALL BASEBALL ETC. ETC.

B.C. TO NOW

HOWARD COSELL,
"IF SOMEONE IS NOT A FORMER ATHLETE
OR A GUTTURAL ILLITERATE, THEN THERE
IS NO ROOM FOR HIM IN THIS BUSINESS."

Sportswriter **Ed Fowler,** *talking about 'Mr. Nice Guy' Chris Schenkel:*

"If Chris were broadcasting World War II, he would thank the Japanese for coming and invite them back."

Don Meredith, *on Monday Night Football:*

"I can't smile and think at the same time."

Bob Costas, *when asked why he still carries two Mickey Mantle baseball cards in his wallet:*

"I believe everyone should carry some type of religious artifact on his or her person at all times."

John Madden, *on quarterback John Elway:*

"He's an instant cure for coaches' burnout."

Los Angeles Clippers broadcaster **Eddie Doucette,** *introducing team owner Donald Sterling:*

"His doctor told him to stay away from crowds, so he went to the Clippers' games."

Joe Garagiola, *talking about catcher Mike Sciosia's ability to block the plate:*

"He's a human dead-end."

Keith Jackson, *during a boxing broadcast:*

"And he goes down for a standing eight count."

Ernie Harwell:

"A sportscaster is a person who can memorize the uniform numbers of 55 players on a college football team but can't remember which dry cleaner has his shirts."

Frank Gifford:

"Pro football is like nuclear warfare. There are no winners, only survivors."

Atlanta broadcaster **Skip Caray,** *talking about horse racing and dog racing:*

"It has always been my philosophy that any sport where you can't interview the winner is not for me."

Earl Weaver, *on his baseball strategy:*

> "My strategy doesn't mean beans. Most nights I could stay home. All I can do as a manager is create situations whereby my players can do what they do best. If they do it, then I'm a genius. If they don't, then Howard Cosell says I'm going against the book. Who wrote that book anyway?"

Golf commentator, after Arnold Palmer put his tee shot at Pebble Beach into the Pacific Ocean:

> "Arnold is entitled to a drop no nearer the hole. But his nearest drop would be in Honolulu."

Los Angeles sportscaster **Jim Hill,** *after unbeaten filly Landaluce scored only a two-length victory in a race at Santa Anita:*

> "It only proves she's human."

Foster Hewitt, *after Eddie Shack of the Toronto Maple Leafs was cut by a high stick and left the ice, blood dripping down his face:*

> "There goes Shack, skating off favoring his forehead."

Football broadcaster **Bob Trumpy,** *talking about Terry Bradshaw late in a close game:*

> "If he can take them 97 yards in two minutes, he ought to play in sandals next week."

Oakland broadcaster **Sam Skinner,** *after the A's played their third 16-inning game:*

> "A's fans don't just buy seats, they lease them."

Football broadcaster **Steve Davis,** *describing a ball carrier who tripped over his own feet:*

> "He was a victim of self-tackleization."

Baseball broadcaster **Ralph Kiner,** *explaining why Richie Allen would never appear on a post-game show:*

> "He said if he came on, all the cold cuts would be gone when he got back to the clubhouse."

Vin Scully, *comparing Alejandro Pena of the Dodgers and Mario Soto of the Reds:*

> "Alejandro's stuff is as good as Mario's but Alejandro is a little eccentric and marches to a different Walkman."

Howard Cosell, *on his decision to avoid political life:*

"Because I'm a public figure, I'm sure I would have been elected. But when I reflect on my life, I'm glad I didn't run for office. As a freshman senator from New York, I would not have had the impact on the American people that I've had."

Tennis commentator **Bud Collins,** *trying to explain an 'unforced error':*

"My Uncle Studley always describes an unforced error as his first marriage."

Joe Garagiola, *on the small glove worn by Cincinnati Reds second baseman Joe Morgan:*

"I know bus drivers with bigger gloves than that."

Bud Harrelson, *on why he was looking forward to his new job as a broadcaster for the New York Mets:*

"As a player and coach, I had to be at the park by 4 p.m. Now I don't have to be there til 7."

Football commentator **Sharon Smith,** *after Dallas Cowboys running back Tony Dorsett broke a 99-yard touchdown run:*

"That's a record that should stand for a long time."

Football broadcaster **Dick Enberg,** *on the possibility that color commentator Merlin Olsen might switch to another network:*

"See these black marks on my lips. That's shoe polish. I've been down on my hands and knees kissing Merlin's shoes, begging him not to leave."

Don Allen, *basketball broadcaster at Southwestern Louisiana University, after the Ragin' Cajuns scored with one second left to narrow the score to 93-77 and then called a time-out:*

"Here comes that 16-point play we've been working on."

Bob Costas, *talking about the Cincinnati Bengals cheerleaders:*

"These are the girl-next-door types — that is, if you happen to live next door to Caesar's Palace."

California Angels owner **Gene Autry,** *on Howard Cosell:*

"Howard calls a great game. It just might not be the one you're watching."

John Madden, *about his casual way of dressing:*

"One day, I was standing outside my apartment and, can you believe it, a bum came up and gave me a dollar."

Atlanta Braves broadcaster **Skip Caray,** *on how he felt during the club's losing streak:*

"Broadcasting those games was like being the entertainment director on the Titanic."

Ernie Harwell:

"A sportscaster is a guy who dresses like Woody Allen, talks like Mel Allen and has a wife who looks like Steve Allen."

Dick Beddoes, *on the poor goaltending of an NHL team:*

"They give exciting impersonations of open windows."

Sportswriter **Red Smith:**

"The Russians have a weapon that can wipe out 280 million Americans. That puts them exactly 10 years behind Howard Cosell."

Football broadcaster **Don Criqui,** *while doing a football game at Buffalo's Rich Stadium where the wind chill factor was below zero degrees fahrenheit:*

"The only people who can survive Buffalo winters are native Buffalonians and other fur-bearing animals."

Sportswriter **Bob Gallas,** *after he was strangled by broadcaster and former player Jimmy Piersall:*

"A guy called me and got on me for hurting Piersall's career. I told him I was very sorry Jimmy had bruised his fingers working on my neck."

John Dennis, *the sports director at WNEV-TV in Boston, after the station hired former Red Sox slugger Carl Yastrzemski:*

"We're not sure exactly what Carl is going to do but one thing we do know, we're going to have a much stronger softball team."

Vin Scully, *on the heat during a game one afternoon:*

"It was so hot today the moon got sunburned."

175

Joe Garagiola, *during a poorly-attended baseball game:*

"Tonight would be a good night to paint the seats."

Bob Uecker, *talking about his career as a player:*

"I once promised this kid in a hospital I'd hit a home run for him. I went 0-for-4 with a couple of strikeouts and the kid had a real bad relapse. It was a really sad story. The thing that bothered me, though, was I found out the kid was only an outpatient anyway."

Frank Gifford, *talking about the lack of recognition received by offensive linemen:*

"Paul Revere got all the credit but he still needed his horse."

Johnny Carson, *after Ron Cey of the Dodgers was beaned during a World Series game:*

"If Cey had been wearing Howard Cosell's toupee, he never would have felt the pitch that hit him."

John Madden:

"NFL quarterbacks are starting to look nervous. That's a nice word for scared."

San Francisco sportscaster **Hank Greenwald,** *celebrating his 50th birthday during a dismal season for the Giants:*

"I don't mind turning 50. It's just that at the beginning of the season I was 43."

Bob Costas, *after eating his second bratwurst in Milwaukee:*

"I've got so much gas that a bunch of Arabs are following me."

Broadcaster **Skip Caray,** *commenting on a crowd of 3,605 in a 19,548-seat facility:*

"It's a partial sellout."

Football broadcaster:

"Anderson has injured his nose. It looks like the same nose he injured last year."

Sportswriter **Jimmy Cannon,** *on Howard Cosell:*

"If Cosell were a sport, he'd be roller derby."

New York Yankees broadcaster **Spencer Ross:**

> "The Oakland A's have just won the rubber game of this four-game series."

Frankie Frisch, *while broadcasting a San Francisco Giants baseball game in windy Candlestick Park:*

> "There's a long drive out to centre field, curving foul."

Don Meredith:

> "If 'ifs' and 'buts' were candy and nuts, we'd all have a Merry Christmas."

Baseball broadcaster **Dizzy Dean,** *after his producer instructed him not to use the word 'guts':*

> "This player has a great deal of intesticle fortitude."

Phyllis George, *when asked how CBS-TV would fill the time if the NFL games were cancelled by a players' strike:*

> "You might see a lot of old Clark Gable movies. Of course, that's not bad."

Pittsburgh Pirates broadcaster **Bob Prince,** *during an extra-inning game in San Francisco which went until midnight local time, or 3 a.m. in Pittsburgh:*

> "There's a ground ball to short, to second for one and on to first for a double play. That's 6-4-3 for those of you scoring in bed."

John Madden, *after quarterback Kenny Stabler threw a low pass for a completion:*

> "When I was coaching Kenny, he'd throw one like that and say: 'Low-ball thrower, highball drinker.' "

Gary Alan Price, *when asked why he calls himself Gary Alan Price:*

> "That's my name."

Bob Costas, *talking about the purity of baseball:*

> "Anyone who thinks it doesn't make a difference whether a game is played in the Astrodome or at Fenway Park likely also doesn't think it makes any difference that Alex Trebek is the host of 'Jeopardy' instead of Art Fleming."

177

Larry King:

"If a sports talk show host talks more than his guest, it's a bad show."

Houston Oilers coach **Bum Phillips,** *talking about the 'no-announcer' game which NBC tried as an experiment:*

"I didn't like it. I'd rather listen to Howard Cosell. At least then you've got something to be mad at."

London sportscaster **Jim Van Horne,** *as two hockey teams prepared to begin sudden-death overtime:*

"The next goal could be a big one."

Vin Scully, *describing how difficult it is to broadcast a golf tournament:*

"It's like being a member of a verbal relay team and you are forever handing off the baton. If all the great statements in history happened in a golf telecast, none of them would ever have been completed. Patrick Henry would have said: 'Give me liberty or — and now let's go to the 16th tee.' "

Ernie Harwell, *remembering the perfect game thrown by Don Larsen in the 1956 World Series:*

"Here the game is over and they're all going wild in Ebbetts Field, and the umpire is down there dusting off the plate for the next batter."

Baseball commentator **Tim McCarver,** *talking about a poor-hitting pitcher:*

"He bats like he pitches — he strands a lot of runners."

Baseball broadcaster, talking about a sparse crowd:

"Either there's hardly anyone here, or a lot of people have come dressed as empty seats."

Sportscaster **Johnny Most,** *on the Boston Celtics:*

"I think as the season progresses you're going to see the Celtics develop some tough, very competitive backgammon players."

Jack Brickhouse, *on the courage of baseball star Enos Slaughter:*

"The guy proved his courage by getting married five times."

Bob Uecker:

"My ultimate desire outside of baseball would be to broadcast wars live. I don't want to open with heavy artillery right away. I'd like to start with spears and knives and things like that."

Frank Gifford, *talking about Monday Night Football:*

"The only trouble we had with Don Meredith was hoping he'd find the right city."

Penn State football coach **Joe Paterno:**

"If I ever need a brain transplant, I hope it comes from a sportswriter because then I'll know it has never been used."

Atlanta Braves broadcaster **Skip Caray,** *as the Chicago Cubs scored five runs in the top of the ninth inning to break a tie:*

"If you folks promise to return for the movie and patronize all our sponsors, you are free to walk the dog right now."

Football broadcaster **George Allen:**

"He made a great play. He kept his body between himself and the ball."

Anonymous colleague, paying a tribute to the positive attitude of St. Louis Blues broadcaster Dan Kelly:

"Kelly is so 'up' on the Blues that if they were all on the Titanic, he'd be talking about what great swimmers they were."

Joe Garagiola, *talking about a long home run ball:*

"That ball travelled eight bucks by cab."

Al Michaels, *calling the final seconds of the U.S. hockey team's gold-medal victory at the Lake Placid Olympics:*

"Do you believe in miracles? Yes!"

Red Smith, *when asked by Howard Cosell how many great sportscasters there are:*

"One fewer than you think, Howard."

CHAPTER 16

OFFICIALS

"Can you get to Seattle by Wednesday?"

Believe it or not, sports officials are human. This story proves the point.

It was during a major league baseball game a few years ago when a runner on first base tried to steal second. The play was extremely close. As the dust flew the **umpire** yelled: 'Safe!' but stood in a definite 'Out' posture. Both the infielder and the runner looked up, somewhat puzzled.

"Well, what am I?" shouted the runner, "safe or out?"

The umpire paused, took a deep breath and then responded.

"You were safe," he said apologetically. "But those 50,000 people in the stands think you're out. I'll get you back later."

With that explanation, the runner quietly left the field.

Former major league umpire **Ron Luciano:**
"I never called a balk in my life. I didn't understand the rule and I still don't. Every time Gene Mauch tried to explain it to me, it got more confusing, so I never bothered with it."

Baltimore Orioles manager **Earl Weaver,** *after umpire Jim Evans told him his eyes were insured for $20,000:*
"What did you do with the money?"

Unknown official:
"Officiating is the only occupation in the world in which the highest accolade is silence."

Houston Oilers coach **Bum Phillips,** *after a game he thought was poorly officiated:*

"I think the NFL should hire full-time officials. If an official can cost me my job, I'd like to be able to cost him his."

Ron Luciano, *on the advantages of retirement:*

"For one thing, now I can wear my glasses in a restaurant when I'm having trouble reading the menu."

Western Mustangs football coach **Larry Haylor,** *following a game he felt was poorly officiated:*

"I thought their (the other team's) officials were better than ours."

American League umpire **Jerry Neudecker:**

"The umpires stay the same. Only the names of the managers change."

NHL referee **Bruce Hood:**

"I have a good way of shutting up a player when he gives me lip. I just say: 'You critique my game and I'll critique yours and we'll see who makes the most mistakes.' They usually have nothing more to say."

Ron Luciano, *to Baltimore manager Earl Weaver:*

"I've got some good news and some bad news. The good news is I'm retiring. The bad news is I'm going to be second-guessing you from the broadcast booth."

Purdue basketball coach **Gene Keady,** *on playing Notre Dame:*

"We'll play them anywhere we can get three good referees who aren't Catholic."

NHL assistant supervisor of officials **John McCauley,** *when asked if coaches and referees would ever get along:*

"No. It won't happen in this lifetime and it won't happen in the next lifetime either because the referees will be up there (pointing up) and the coaches will be down there (pointing down)."

Umpire, to a group of angry players:

"I'm not arguing with all of you. Who's your designated loudmouth?"

American League P.R. person **Phyllis Merhige,** *after some off-color remarks at a New York City baseball dinner:*
"I wasn't offended. I don't shock easily. I read the umpires' reports, you know."

NBA referee **Earl Strom,** *after calling the foul on which Houston's Elvin Hayes set the career record for fouls committed:*
"I felt like stopping the game and giving him my whistle."

Ron Luciano:
"It's a little-known fact that Boog Powell was really one of the Alou brothers but he got tired of being called Boog Alou."

NBA referee **Ed Rush,** *on the requirements he needed to get his job:*
"Can you run, can you see, can you read the rules and can you get to Seattle by Wednesday?"

Gordie Howe, *offering a compliment of sorts to an official:*
"You are the second-best referee I've ever seen. All the rest are tied for first."

Ron Luciano:
"Earl Weaver was a great manager. I just couldn't stand him, absolutely couldn't stand him. You might say we had an intense personality conflict. He was too short for one thing."

Retired umpire **Ed Vargo,** *after watching some games from the stands and listening to the fans:*
"There is no way I could call balls and strikes from those seats. For one thing, the umpire's in the way."

NHL referee **Vern Buffey,** *when asked how he decides if a spear should be a minor penalty or a major penalty:*
"It depends on whether the stick comes out the other side."

Utah Jazz centre **Mark Eaton,** *when told by his coach to stay out of foul trouble:*
"Fine with me, tell the refs."

American League umpire **Bill Kunkel,** *on the problem he would face if he had to umpire a game in which his son Jeff was playing:*

"If I gave him ball four, everyone would say I was showing favoritism. If I struck him out, my wife would immediately change all the padlocks on the house."

Ron Luciano, *on his plans for retirement:*

"I plan to yell at umpires a lot. I want to keep my hand in the game."

Anonymous fan, to a basketball referee:

"Hey ref, if you had another eye you'd be a cyclops."

Basketball referee **Irv Brown,** *on former Marquette coach Al McGuire:*

"He always wanted a technical foul early in the game. It was part of his ploy to work the crowd. The maddest I ever saw him was when I gave Bobby Knight a 'T' before him."

Kansas City Royals third baseman **George Brett,** *following the famous 'pine tar' incident:*

"I told that umpire everything my father used to tell me when I brought home my report card."

Vanderbilt assistant coach **Dale Clayton,** *on basketball's three-referee system:*

"It just gives you one more to yell at."

Umpire **Pam Postma,** *explaining why she ejected a certain player from the ball game:*

"I could take being called a 'blankety-blank.' That didn't bother me. But when he called me a 'blinkety-blank' he was history."

Hockey referee **Mickey Ion:**

"There are 14,000 people in the building but only one sane person — me."

Major league umpire **Ken Kaiser,** *on Maury Wills when Wills was the manager of the Seattle Mariners:*

"Wills is absolutely the worst manager I've ever seen. He doesn't even know how to argue."

Football referee, to the captain who won the coin toss:
> "Okay, you have your choice — receiving or facing the TV cameras."

Ron Luciano, *on his battles with Earl Weaver:*
> "Earl and I had dinner last Sunday. He was in Florida and I was in New York but we both ate at 6:30. That's the closest we'll ever get."

Oakland A's manager **Billy Martin,** *talking about umpire Jerry Neudecker:*
> "He's so incompetent that he couldn't be a crew chief on a sunken submarine."

Milwaukee Bucks coach **Don Nelson,** *on referee Earl Strom:*
> "Earl once called a three-second violation with 22 seconds left on the 24-second clock."

Bum Phillips, *coach of the South team, after a controversial call caused his team to lose the Senior Bowl 14-6 to the North:*
> "Now I know why we lost the Civil War. We had the same officials."

Atlanta Braves broadcaster **Skip Caray,** *on hefty umpire Eric Gregg:*
> "When Eric hits the deck, the deck comes out second best."

Bob Bailey, *the sheriff of Cabell County, W.Va., explaining why he named Marshall University basketball coach Rick Huckabay an honorary deputy:*
> "That's so the next time Southern Conference officials come in here and rob you, you can take them to jail yourself."

Milwaukee Brewers manager **George Bamberger,** *talking about the umpires in a particular game:*
> "The only guy who didn't mess up was the guy on third but he had no calls. If he would have had any, he probably would have messed it up to make a full house."

DePaul basketball coach **Ray Meyer:**
> "My ultimate goal is to referee a game played by officials."

Anonymous:

"The coach's job is to teach, the official's job is to arbitrate. Neither should encroach on the other's duties."

Former NFL referee **Norm Schachter,** *on pre-game coin flips:*

"Vince Lombardi always called tails. He thought that side was heavier."

Ron Luciano, *on his book:*

"Since ballplayers can't read, I put it on cassette so they can listen on those headphones they wear. I also printed it in braille so umpires can read it."

NHL referee **Ron Wicks,** *when asked about the most important qualities an official should have:*

"A short memory and a sense of humor."

University of Maryland basketball coach **Lefty Driesell,** *after his team returned from an overseas tour:*

"I liked the officials. They couldn't understand a word I was saying."

American League supervisor of umpires **Dick Butler,** *on the language which sometimes takes place on the field:*

"If you took three words out of the English language, most players and umpires would be mute."

Veteran basketball referee **Leo Perrone:**

"A lady in the stands said she'd pray for a miracle so my sight would be restored."

Unknown baseball fan:

"Umpires eat rhubarb pie for dessert."

CHAPTER 17

SPORTS EXECUTIVES

"It fouls up our playoff rotation."

When it comes to dealing with sports executives, every member of the media has at least one good story. My story is about former Toronto Blue Jays president, **Peter Bavasi**.

It was mid-September, 1979, and the Blue Jays were nearing the end of their third season. The team finished last in each of those years. There was increasing speculation manager Roy Hartsfield was going to be replaced by Atlanta Braves manager Bobby Cox. Peter Bavasi was my guest on the radio talk show and I intended to press him for confirmation of that speculation. However, Mr. Bavasi was not about to tip his hand.

GAP: "Peter, I wish I could get you to commit yourself to Bobby Cox but obviously you're not going to do that."

BAVASI: "I'll commit myself to this extent. Bobby Cox will not manage our ball club, period."

GAP: "Will Roy Hartsfield be your manager next season?"

BAVASI: "I'm not in a position to make that decision as yet."

GAP: "Peter, I coached a peewee team this summer, so maybe...."

BAVASI: "Well, then I'm going to put your name in the cropper with everyone else, just in case a change is ever made."

GAP: "But, just a second, my team ended last."

BAVASI: "Then you're qualified for the job."

New York Yankees owner **George Steinbrenner:**

"Sportswriters are always describing how I barge into the locker room. I never barge in. I'm always waiting there when they come through the door."

CFL commissioner **Jake Gaudaur:**

"Those like me who were born in the 1920s have seen it all — feast, famine, war, brilliance, stupidity — and that's only in the CFL."

Oakland A's owner **Charlie Finley,** on baseball commissioner Bowie Kuhn:

"I've often called Bowie Kuhn the village idiot but I want to apologize to all the village idiots of America. He's the nation's idiot."

Hamilton Tiger-Cats owner **Harold Ballard,** after a win over Toronto:

"Maybe I'll have to buy the Argos and make them a farm team."

Atlanta Braves owner **Ted Turner,** when a reporter suggested his team made a good tax shelter:

"They're a shelter all right — a bomb shelter."

U. S. President **Gerald Ford:**

"I had pro offers from the Detroit Lions and the Green Bay Packers, who were pretty hard up for linemen in those days. If I had gone into pro football, my name might have been a household word today."

Bill Veeck, when asked during his retirement if he missed owning a major league baseball team:

"No, because now I can watch the games without the heartache. When a guy misses a fly ball, it gives me great relief to know I'm not the one paying him $600,000 a year."

Chicago Cubs owner **Phil Wrigley,** on baseball:

"It's the only business I know of where you go to your competitors for help."

Los Angeles Express owner **Alan Harmon,** explaining how the team colors were chosen:

"We took the silver from Detroit, the blue from Dallas and the burgundy from my daughter's blouse."

George Steinbrenner, *commenting on inter-league play:*

"Let's put it this way. I'd love to play the Mets more and the Red Sox less."

Comedian **Argus Hamilton,** *after attending a California Angels game which was also attended by former U.S. President Nixon:*

"Apprehension is ordering a hot dog and passing a $20 bill down the row past Richard Nixon."

Indiana Pacers public relations director **Ray Compton,** *on the club's small crowds:*

"Our season was a disaster. The muggers downtown were filing for unemployment because there was no one to mug."

Buzzie Bavasi, *on the large crowds at Dodger Stadium:*

"In L.A., 20,000 people show up just to see why the lights are on."

Philadelphia 76ers general manager **Pat Williams:**

"When they finally read the list of great basketball coaches, Frank Layden will be there — listening."

Los Angeles Rams executive **Dick Beam,** *talking about one of the club's coaches:*

"Football is in his blood. His red corpuscles are actually shaped like little footballs."

Johnny Carson, *after the California Angels blew a playoff series to Milwaukee:*

"Angels owner Gene Autry has been in touch with Roy Rogers. He wants to know how to stuff an entire baseball team."

Dallas Cowboys general manager **Tex Schramm,** *talking about the great success of his organization, both on and off the field:*

"I would say the reason we have done so much is because of the importance of people. I can't stress that enough."

Calvin Griffith, *when asked about his future plans after selling the Minnesota Twins:*

"I plan to be a good-time Charlie."

Montreal Expos farm director **Jim Fanning,** *who spent his honeymoon on a scouting trip in the Caribbean:*

"The first two things I bought my wife were a stopwatch and a clipboard."

Cleveland Cavaliers owner **Ted Stepien,** *on why he wanted to sell the team:*

"Then I'll be able to watch them play each game for $18 instead of $100,000."

Former baseball slugger **Ken Harrelson,** *talking about one of his biggest mistakes:*

"When they first came out, I bought 17 Nehru jackets. But that fad lasted about as long as my longest hitting streak, eight days. Know anybody who wants a good used Nehru jacket?"

San Diego Clippers owner **Donald Sterling,** *on rumors he was looking for co-owners:*

"Nobody's as stupid as me. Nobody's going to invest in this team."

Stanton Cook *of the Chicago Tribune, when asked if Wrigley Field would be getting lights:*

"I can't shed any light on that."

George Steinbrenner:

"Owning the Yankees is unique. I've had some big offers to sell the team. No way. Owning the Yankees is like owning the Mona Lisa."

Connie Mack, *on his retirement from baseball at the age of 88:*

"I'm not quitting because I'm too old. I'm quitting because I think people want me to quit."

Bill Veeck, *on why he sold the Chicago White Sox:*

"It wasn't the high price of the stars, it was the high price of the mediocrity."

Cleveland Browns owner **Art Modell,** *after a 5-11 season:*

"There is absolutely no truth to the rumor that the Browns highlight film will be a Polaroid shot."

Comedian **Jackie Kahane,** *at a roast for Philadelphia Phillies manager Dallas Green:*

"Dallas Green, great name for a white guy. Sounds like a golf course in Texas."

Los Angeles Raiders owner **Al Davis,** *on his long feud with NFL commissioner Pete Rozelle:*

"If Richard Nixon had had Pete Rozelle's public relations staff, he'd still be president."

Former baseball great **Jimmy Piersall,** *talking about Charlie Finley:*

"I'm going to write a book about my days with Finley and I'm going to call it 'And They Thought I was Crazy.'"

CFL executive **Herb Capozzi,** *talking about Hamilton Tiger-Cats fans:*

"They're dressed beautifully. They sit there in black leather jackets, T-shirts advertising a beer, caps with tire company advertising and they have tattoos all over their forearms. The men aren't dressed badly either."

Atlanta Braves owner **Ted Turner,** *responding to criticism about the high salaries of his players:*

"At my stupidest, I was never as stupid as the Boston Red Sox."

Former baseball commissioner **Happy Chandler,** *opening the Hall of Fame induction ceremonies:*

"I feel like the mosquito who flew into the nudist camp — I don't know where to start."

St. Louis broadcaster **Jack Buck,** *on the new yacht bought by George Steinbrenner:*

"It's a beautiful thing to behold, with all 36 oars working in unison."

Hamilton Tiger-Cats owner **Harold Ballard,** *when he hired Frank Kush as coach:*

"He's not going to be one of those coaches who come into the dressing room and throw Bibles around and get the players thinking of religion instead of football."

Former Hamilton Tiger-Cats coach **Jim Trimble,** *talking about general manager Ralph Sazio:*

"He throws nickels around like manhole covers."

Baltimore Orioles director of player development **Tom Giordano,** *on why teams don't scout in Europe or Africa:*

"By the time you found a guy and taught him to play the game, he'd be eligible for free agency."

Sportswriter **Jim Murray:**

"I know lots of people who were surprised when Bowie Kuhn got fired. They didn't know he had a job."

Chicago White Sox owner **Bill Veeck,** *on the reason for his headaches:*

"I got more headaches chasing Luis Aparicio all over Venezuela."

Al Davis, *talking about his L.A. Raiders:*

"Everyone else says: 'We'll take what the defence gives us.' On the Raiders, we take what we want."

Houston Astros owner **John McMullen:**

"Nothing is more limited than being a limited partner to George Steinbrenner."

Frankie Frisch, *on baseball:*

"You haven't seen the whole ball game unless you've seen every pitch."

Ed Garvey, *when he resigned as the head of the NFL Players Association to return to his law practice in Wisconsin:*

"Now I can finally admit that I'm a Green Bay Packers fan."

Ted Turner, *shortly after signing outfielder Claudell Washington to a five-year contract worth somewhere near $3.5 million:*

"Baseball owners must work together to lower major league salaries."

Chicago Cubs P.R. man **Ned Colletti,** *after the season opener was rained out:*

"It fouls up our playoff rotation."

GEORGE STEINBRENNER, JUST AFTER HE BOUGHT THE YANKEES IN 1973:

"WE PLAN ABSENTEE OWNERSHIP, WE'RE NOT GOING TO PRETEND TO BE SOMETHING WE AREN'T. I'LL STICK TO BUILDING SHIPS."

Gene Corrigan, *after he was named athletic director at Notre Dame:*

"There's an old saying that the second son of an Irish family should become a priest. This job is as close as I'll come."

Vida Blue, *a member of the Oakland A's championship teams:*

"I wonder if Charlie Finley is ever going to have a reunion of all those players. I doubt it. He wouldn't want to pay for all those hotel rooms."

Philadelphia 76ers general manager **Pat Williams:**

"Basketball is the one sport that can truly be influenced by one man. Baseball and football can't and hockey no one understands anyway."

Dodgers owner **Walter O'Malley,** *as he announced the hiring of Walter Alston as manager:*

"This is Walter Alston. I have hired him to beat the Yankees next year."

Dallas Cowboys player personnel director **Gil Brandt,** *on the problems of judging college talent:*

"It's easy to pick out the top 10 per cent and the bottom 10 per cent. It's the 80 per cent in the middle that looks the same."

George Steinbrenner, *explaining why he prefers thoroughbreds to baseball players:*

"Because they can't talk to sportswriters."

Chicago Bears lineman **Dan Jiggetts,** *talking about team owner George Halas:*

"When Mr. Halas tells you what time it is, you don't have to look at your watch."

Former U.S. Secretary of State **Henry Kissinger,** *after he tried unsuccessfully to secure the 1986 World Cup of soccer for the United States:*

"My dealings with FIFA over the World Cup have made me nostalgic for the Middle East."

Bill Veeck, *who once sent a midget to the plate as a pinch-hitter:*

"I'll always be remembered for that. In fact, I wouldn't mind if they put on my tombstone: 'He helped the little man.' "

Detroit Pistons coach **Scotty Robertson,** *when asked if he wanted general manager Jack McCloskey to call heads or tails in the coin flip to determine the first selection in the NBA draft:*

"I have no preference. That's his job."

Minnesota Twins executive vice-president **Clark Griffith Jr.:**

"We took a survey of our fans that showed they like a lot of home runs. So we built a pitching staff to accommodate them."

Dallas Mavericks player personnel director **Rick Sund,** *during a particularly poor season:*

"I stopped at the toll booth on my way to work this morning, tossed my only quarter at the basket — and shot an air ball. The guard looked at me and said: 'You must work for the Mavericks.' "

Ted Turner:

"When I bought the Braves six years ago, I did not know what the infield fly rule was and I'm not sure I know what it is now."

Baseball executive **Branch Rickey:**

"Hitting a ball and scoring a run are, in a way, what all of us try to do all our lives. Baseball becomes a symbol, win or lose, and the romance never really ends."

Yankees outfielder **Dave Collins,** *on George Steinbrenner:*

"If we lose eight or nine games in a row, I'm sure not going to jump into the same elevator with him."

Houston Oilers owner **Bud Adams:**

"If the Astrodome is the eighth wonder of the world, the rent is the ninth."

Boston Celtics general manager **Red Auerbach,** *on basketball:*

"The ball is round and the floor is smooth — no problem."

NBC executive producer **Michael Weisman,** *on his decision not to televise the traditional phone call from the president after the Super Bowl game:*

"All I know is I just got a call from the IRS and they want my last five years of income-tax returns."

Chicago White Sox operations director **Ken Harrelson,** *on his efforts to hire a general manager for the team:*

"I want to fill the job so I can fire someone when I mess up."

Washington Bullets general manager **Bob Ferry,** *commenting on the number of groin injuries in the NBA:*

"I can't understand it. We never had pulled groins when I played and we had groins."

William E. Simon, *after giving up his efforts to buy the Baltimore Orioles:*

"It's a dead deal and cannot be resurrected. It's awfully difficult to reheat old mashed potatoes."

Illinois Senator **John F. Dunn,** *on noise pollution at Wrigley Field in Chicago:*

"Noise pollution at Wrigley Field can't be much of a problem. With the Cubs there, there's nothing to cheer about."

Oakland A's pitcher **Steve McCatty,** *on former team owner Charlie Finley:*

"When Charlie had his heart operation, it took eight hours — 7 1/2 just to find his heart."

CFL executive **Herb Capozzi,** *talking about commissioner Jake Gaudaur, who had been a rowing champion:*

"Rowing is the only sport in which you sit on your fanny backward and expect to win."

Philadelphia 76ers general manager **Pat Williams,** *poking fun at a university basketball program:*

"They had a big scandal at this place. Three players were found in the library."

Oakland A's president **Roy Eisenhardt:**

"Watching baseball in a domed stadium is like listening to music with ear muffs on."

Toronto Blue Jays president **Peter Bavasi,** *discussing the expansion team's marketing strategy:*

"We're not selling the steak. We're selling the sizzle."

George Steinbrenner, *after Lou Piniella challenged the team rule about long hair by saying that he was simply emulating Jesus Christ:*

"Lou, as soon as you can walk on water, you can wear your hair any way you want."

Baseball commissioner **Bowie Kuhn,** *after watching a World Series game in 38-degree fahrenheit weather in Cincinnati:*

"I did not wear my topcoat because I wanted to show the fans that it wasn't really that cold. I nearly froze my arse off."

CHAPTER 18

MONEY

"It's another seven bucks for the costumes."

When Pete Rose was a free agent in 1978, he decided to sign with the Philadelphia Phillies. However, it must have been a tough decision.

There were several teams interested in Pete's services, including the Roundtable II Pizza softball team of Rancho Bernardo, Calif. In a telegram to Rose, the club made a substantial offer. The deal included a red and white uniform, his choice of third base or outfield and all the beer he could drink.

To show his good faith, the manager ended the telegram by saying: "This offer is flexible. We are willing to negotiate."

Los Angeles Dodgers manager **Tommy Lasorda,** *about the big contract signed by pitcher Fernando Valenzuela:*
> "Today he's earning a million dollars a year. Three years ago, the guy's alarm clock was a rooster."

Lou Holtz, *on a coach's job security:*
> "A lifetime contract for a coach means that if you're ahead in the third quarter and are moving the ball, they can't fire you."

North Carolina State basketball coach **Jim Valvano,** *when asked what changes he'd like to see in the game:*
> "I'd like to see all Italian coaches get lifetime contracts."

Chicago Cubs **Leo Durocher,** *on the security of managing a major league baseball team:*
> "If you lose, you're going to be fired, and if you win, you only put off the day you're going to be fired."

Former NFL great **Sam Huff,** *when asked to give some advice to current players:*

"An amazing thing happens when you quit. Your paycheques stop coming."

Pete Rose:

"With the money I'm making, I should be playing two positions."

University of Florida linebacker **Wilber Marshall,** *talking about the fact that he babysits in his spare time:*

"My only fee is an open refrigerator."

Beasley Reece, *explaining how he became the New York Giants player representative:*

"It was like something out of an Abbott and Costello movie. They lined everybody up and said: 'All those who want to be player rep, take one step forward.' Everybody took a step backward but me."

California Angels president **Buzzie Bavasi,** *on the salary structure in baseball:*

"I hope we're not at the point where players who make $700,000 and $800,000 feel unwanted."

Eddie Edwards *of the Cincinnati Bengals, when asked his motivation for winning the division title:*

"Feeling good and 10 grand."

Fenway Park concessionaire **Harry Stevens,** *after the Boston Red Sox lost catcher Carlton Fisk to the Chicago White Sox:*

"That will cost our operation at least $200,000. Fisk used to visit the pitcher at least twice an inning and that's when the fans would do their concession buying."

Former CFL player **Vince Mazza:**

"Everybody says the football player of today is faster, stronger and smarter than we ever were. If that's the truth, how come they wear pantyhose and need agents?"

Sports agent **Mike Trope,** *on his negotiating style:*

"I'm willing to be reasonable but I'm also inflexible."

Terry Bogener, *an outfielder for the Charleston Charlies of the International League, talking about his salary:*

> "Everybody thinks ball players make big money. If people knew what I was making, they'd invite me out to dinner."

Dan Reeves, *when asked what it meant to be both vice-president and head coach of the Denver Broncos:*

> "It means I can be fired from two jobs instead of one."

Bruce Sokol, *a friend of Texas A&M football coach Jackie Sherrill:*

> "Ten years ago, Jackie told me his goal was to be the head coach at a major university. Now he says his goal is to own a major university."

Former Cincinnati Bengals tight end **Bob Trumpy,** *on the security of college coaching:*

> "Contracts for college coaches should be written on the beach at low tide."

Basketball scout **Joe Lapchick,** *raving about high school player Lew Alcindor, who later became Kareem Abdul-Jabbar:*

> "He could become the greatest player ever. Someday the pros will have to pay him $50,000 a year."

NFL coach **George Allen:**

> "Politicians get canned and write books. Football coaches get canned and become columnists."

Montreal Expos **Bill Lee,** *explaining why he sent a cheque for $251 when commissioner Bowie Kuhn had fined him only $250:*

> "I want him to know I'm worth more than he thinks and I want to screw up the accounting."

Baltimore Colts quarterback **Bert Jones,** *talking about his plans after retirement:*

> "I'd like to be an entrepreneur. They threw that word around in economics at college and I always wondered what it meant."

Basketball coach **Cotton Fitzsimmons,** *when asked how long his new contract was:*
"About five pages."

Anonymous:
"After you get all decked out for skiing, your wallet offers little to fall back on."

Will Rogers:
"College athletes ask me: 'When should I turn pro?' And I tell them: 'Not until you've earned all the money you can in college.' "

Pete Rose:
"I love this game so much I would play it for nothing."

Edmonton Eskimos **Dan Kepley,** *before a game against the Montreal Alouettes and highly-paid quarterback Vince Ferragamo:*
"I think I'm going to enjoy this game. I've never hit a million dollars before."

Reggie Jackson, *putting his contract talks into perspective:*
"Everything takes care of itself if you hit the ball over the wall."

Gordie Howe, *talking about the financial success of the World Hockey Association:*
"With the exception of the teams going bankrupt, our league has never been in better shape."

Frank Kush, *on the coaching adjustments he expects to make in going from college football to pro football:*
"Instead of slapping helmets, I'll slap wallets."

Dallas sportswriter **Blackie Sherrod,** *on the sale of the Cowboys:*
"The Dallas Cowboys cheerleaders are included in the $60-million asking price. However, if you also want their costumes, it will be another seven bucks."

California Angels general manager **Buzzie Bavasi:**
"The way salaries are skyrocketing, it won't be long before the teams take out loans from the players."

Abe Collinsworth, *father of receiver Cris Collinsworth, after Cris turned pro with the Cincinnati Bengals:*

"The biggest change in Cris is the price of his Christmas gifts. This year, his mother and I got a trip to Hawaii instead of that blamed necktie he gave me last year."

Rangers coach **Herb Brooks,** *talking about his first experience with New York:*

"Some guy stole my wife's American Express card but I decided not to report it because the guy spent $200 a month less than my wife did."

Maria Trillo, *who handles all of the contract negotiations for her husband, Manny:*

"Some agents get 10 per cent, others get 15 per cent. I get it all and I know how to spend it."

Kansas City Kings general manager **Joe Axelson,** *commenting on a contract signed by a certain player:*

"He's got a deal that makes the Magna Carta look like a roll of toilet paper."

Tampa Bay Buccaneers quarterback **Steve Young,** *on the difference between the NFL and the USFL:*

"Now, we don't have to chip in to pay the bus driver to get us to the airport."

Sportswriter **Hubert Mizell,** *on the 850-page contract signed by San Diego Chargers quarterback Dan Fouts:*

"It's longer than the U.S. Constitution, the Magna Carta, the Ten Commandments, the Declaration of Independence and the Sunday St. Petersburg Times all combined."

Philadelphia Flyers defenceman **Frank Bathe:**

"My accountant won't let me incorporate. He says the last thing this country needs is another poor company."

Oakland A's president **Roy Eisenhardt,** *talking about the contract he gave to new manager Steve Boros:*

"Steve has the same kind of contract I have. It runs 20 years if he does a good job and 20 days if he doesn't."

Jack Elway, *after his quarterback son John received a $140,000 signing bonus:*

"It's a great summer job for John. Now he'll be able to buy a second pair of shoes."

Carl Erskine, *when asked why he shows up at Los Angeles Dodgers oldtimer games every year:*

"With expenses and everything, they've paid me more than I made when I was pitching."

Boston Celtics coach **Bill Fitch,** *on his financial situation:*

"I am independently wealthy. I have enough money to last me the rest of my life — providing I die tomorrow."

Pete Rose, *when asked about his reflexes after he turned 40:*

"My reflexes are still good and even if they go I've got enough money to buy some new ones."

Bill Flynn, *athletic director at Boston College, after his $40,000-a-year coach Jack Bicknell upset Texas A&M coach Jackie Sherrill at $250,000:*

"I'm waiting for Jack to come in here and ask for a big raise."

Dodgers general manager **Al Campanis,** *after the signing of Fernando Valenzuela:*

"This is truly an international event. We signed an outstanding Mexican pitcher at an Italian restaurant in Chinatown."

Minnesota Twins owner **Calvin Griffith,** *when asked to speculate on where Billy Martin would be the next season:*

"He may end up in Sing Sing if he doesn't pay the $100,000 he owes the IRS."

Comedian **David Letterman,** *describing the scene when the verdict in the USFL's lawsuit against the NFL was handed down:*

"There were 150 people in the courtroom, the third largest crowd ever to see the USFL in action."

Ralph Kiner, *talking about his semi-pro baseball days:*

"I got one dollar a game and an extra fifty cents for hitting a home run."

San Diego State basketball coach **Smokey Gaines:**

"Michael Cage is a special kind of kid. He's the kind of kid I'd want for my own son. I'd want him for my own son because one day he's going to make a lot of money."

Mrs. George Burns, *calling the UPI sports department to find out how her husband did in a golf tournament:*

"How much money did he make?"

Portland Beavers general manager **Dave Hersh,** *after signing veteran pitcher Luis Tiant:*

"Luis spent the morning undergoing a medical examination and the doctor tells me Luis is in excellent financial condition."

Former NFL star **Bobby Layne:**

"We had more fun on our money than the guys today are having on theirs."

California Angels infielder **Bobby Grich:**

"The bad thing about baseball is all the travel you do. You go to all those big cities and all you tend to do is shop. The good thing is you can afford it."

Lou Holtz, *at the beginning of one football season:*

"This is what I call a replacement year. That means if we don't do well, the coach gets replaced."

Oklahoma coach **Barry Switzer,** *on the perils of his job:*

"Football coaching is like a terminal disease. It's going to get you sooner or later, you just don't know when."

Lee Corso, *on what he did to occupy his time after he was fired as football coach at the University of Indiana:*

"I've cleaned my basement 14 times. I have the cleanest basement in America."

Oklahoma City basketball coach **Abe Lemons:**

"When I started, we used to make very little money and have a lot of fun. Now we make lots of money and have no fun at all. I like it better this way."

Former Denver Broncos coach **John Ralston,** *explaining that he was fired because of illness and fatigue:*

"The fans were sick and tired of me."

Kansas City first baseman **Pete LaCock,** *explaining why the Royals should give him a new contract with a big raise:*

"I've got a lot of things going for me. I do a lot of work for the Cancer Society in the city and my father gives Kansas City a lot of publicity." (LaCock's father, Peter Marshall, was host of the popular game show 'Hollywood Squares.')

Stan Musial, *after Pete Rose signed with Philadelphia:*

"Pete doesn't count his money any more. He weighs it."

B. C. Lions linebacker **Ray Nettles,** *on his contract:*

"I just told my agent to get off his butt and get working on my new contract. He knows he's not dealing with an ordinary human being. If I don't get action, I'll blow up his office."

Houston Astros general manager **Al Rosen,** *talking about clauses in the player contracts which limit certain physical activities while out of uniform:*

"About the most strenuous thing we allow them to do is get in and out of bed."

Mike Scioscia, *on his contract talks with the Los Angeles Dodgers:*

"We were 60 bucks apart and they weren't budging. Then it was 40 bucks and at last it was 20. Finally they decided that I didn't have to clean out the locker room. I didn't get the money I wanted but the fringe benefits are outstanding."

Cliff Stoudt, *after three seasons of serving as Pittsburgh Steelers back-up quarterback:*

"I think I deserve a raise. I mean, I save them money on cleaning bills."

Billy Sims, *as a highly-paid rookie running back with the Detroit Lions, introducing himself to the veteran players:*

"Hi, fellas. I'm Billy Sims from the University of Oklahoma. I'm the reason most of you guys haven't got raises."

BASEBALL GREAT **BABE RUTH**, WHEN
INFORMED THAT HE HAD A HIGHER SALARY
THAN U.S. PRESIDENT CALVIN COOLIDGE :

"THAT'S UNDERSTANDABLE BECAUSE I
HAD A BETTER YEAR."

Steve Stone, *as a member of the Baltimore Orioles pitching staff, talking about his 1968 Chatham team in the Cape Cod League:*

"Thurman Munson got $135,000 from the Yankees, John Curtis got $100,000 from the Red Sox, Bobby Valentine got $65,000 from the Dodgers, Rich McKinney got $35,000 from the White Sox and all I got was mono and hepatitis."

Los Angeles Dodgers pitcher **Don Sutton:**

"I'm the most loyal player money can buy."

Edward Bennett Williams, *talking about George Allen:*

"I gave George an unlimited expense account and he exceeded it."

Agent **Bob Woolf,** *after negotiating a $175,000 contract for female basketball player Carol Blazejowski:*

"It's the first time a client has ever kissed me goodbye."

Joe DiMaggio, *estimating the kind of money he would make in today's free agent market:*

"If I were sitting down with George Steinbrenner and based on what Dave Winfield got for his statistics, I'd have to say: 'George, you and I are about to become partners.' "

Kansas City Kings general manager **Joe Axelson,** *commenting on his salary:*

"It's a typical NBA contract. It pays me about four times what I'm worth."

San Francisco Giants pitcher **Greg Minton,** *on his big-money contract:*

"It specifies that I can do no water, snow, or cross-country skiing. No motorcycles. No roller skating. No hang gliding. No basketball. Furthermore, there's no touch or flag football. No pro rodeo tour. No sky diving. No skateboards. It even says no ice hockey and I've never been on skates in my life."

Philadelphia Phillies pitcher **Tug McGraw,** *talking about plans for his World Series money:*

"Ninety per cent of it I'll spend on whiskey, women and other good times. The other 10 per cent I'll probably waste."

Bob Valvano, *basketball coach at Kutztown State College in Pennsylvania, on whether he is ever mistaken for his more famous brother Jim, the coach at North Carolina State:*

"Just have them meet me on the first or 15th of the month. Then there will be no doubt which Valvano is which."

Alyce Bartberger, *the aunt of Pittsburgh Pirates manager Chuck Tanner, after she won $2.5 million in the Pennsylvania lottery:*

"I'm going to buy half a player for Chuck. At today's prices, that's all I can afford."

Bill Bates *of the Dallas Cowboys, when asked what he would do if he ever had a chance to buy the team:*

"Give Bill Bates a big raise."

Buzzie Bavasi, *after the Angels signed Reggie Jackson to a hefty contract and season-ticket sales doubled:*

"Reggie paid for his whole contract in one week."

New England Patriots coach **Ron Erhardt,** *talking about fines collected from the players after a brawl with the New York Jets:*

"It goes to a good cause, the coaches' retirement fund. That's why, when the fight started, I waved the whole squad onto the field."

Grand Prix promoter **Ralph Sanchez,** *following an event which lost $800,000:*

"I consider this one of the biggest successes of my career."

Jay Johnstone, *of the Los Angeles Dodgers, after Fernando Valenzuela rejoined the team following a contract dispute:*

"He's fat, he has pimples all over his face, he can't speak English and he's ugly. Yes, we're glad to have him back."

Montreal Canadiens forward **Peter Mahovlich,** *after the Parti Quebecois won the provincial election:*

"Do we get paid in dollars or francs?"

Pete Rose, *shortly after he signed for $800,000 a year with the Philadelphia Phillies:*

"I know the buck isn't what it used to be but do you realize I had to put in seven big years to reach six figures."

Banner at Busch Stadium in St. Louis:

"Hi Kids. Send money. Love Mom."

Minnesota Twins manager **Billy Gardner,** *on team owner Carl Pohlad:*

"I hear he's so rich he bought his dog a boy."

Yogi Berra, *on the cost of living:*

"A nickel ain't worth a dime any more."

Pro golfer **Kathy Horvath:**

"When I was growing up, I wanted to be a neurosurgeon and even though some people think I haven't done much since I turned pro, I'd have to be a darn good surgeon to make what I'm making."

Minnesota Twins scout **Ellis Clary,** *on the team's low payroll:*

"We've got the only players who can make more in World Series shares than they make in their salaries."

Golf analyst **John Brodie,** *explaining his decision to leave golf and pursue a career in football:*

"I was a pro golfer for a while in 1959. I was the leading money-spender on the tour."

Tommy Lasorda, *talking about his contract:*

"It's a multi-month deal."

NHL great **Tim Horton,** *after he signed a new contract:*

"They pay me to practise. I'd play the games for nothing."

Minnesota Twins owner **Calvin Griffith:**

"I haven't had a pay raise in over three years but then again I don't need a pay raise because I'm not into fancy stuff. One thing, though, I've noticed that I'm getting $100 less per day than I did earlier this year. I don't know why but I'm going to find out."

Hockey agent **Larry Rauch,** *talking about some difficult contract negotiations:*

"In trade talks, they talk about my client like he's filet mignon. In contract talks, he's veal chops."

Brigham Young centre **Trevor Matich,** *who snapped the ball for Steve Young during their college careers:*

> "If Steve Young's hands are worth $40 million, I wonder how much my rear end would go for?"

Sportswriter **Blackie Sherrod,** *responding to a comment by Atlanta Braves owner Ted Turner that salaries were too high:*

> "That's like Al Capone speaking out for gun control."

CHAPTER 19

WINNING AND LOSING

"We just got our booties blown off."

Like every father who has ever played games with his kids, I know the agony of perpetual defeat. Let's face it, dads simply cannot beat kids at kids' games, or even most adult games.

So it was one day as I finished a game of cards with my six-year-old daughter **Dana**. She sat across the table with all the cards in hand and a big proud smile on her face. I sat there empty-handed and tried to push a graceful grin across my lips.

"You're the winner again," I sighed, "and I'm the loser."

"You're not the loser, Daddy," she declared with youthful enthusiasm. "You're the second winner."

I like the concept.

Arkansas football coach **Lou Holtz,** *after a 6-5 season:*
"I'm two steps ahead of the posse and one step from suicide."

Calgary Flames coach **Bob Johnson,** *after the team's 10th straight loss:*
"We're in a slump because everybody tells us we're in a slump."

Buffalo Bills coach **Hank Bullough,** *on his team's problems:*
"We keep beating ourselves but we're getting better at it."

Philadelphia Eagles quarterback **Ron Jaworski,** *on aging:*
"When you're winning, you're experienced. When you're losing, you're old."

New York Islanders goaltender **Chico Resch:**
"The difference between winning and losing is 10 miles per hour. When you're losing, you drive to the rink at 50-to-55 miles an hour. When you're winning, you go 60-to-65, because you can't wait to get there."

Cincinnati Bengals receiver **Cris Collinsworth,** *after the club lost its season-opener:*
"It's okay, 15-1 should still win our division."

Pittsburgh Steelers receiver **Lynn Swann,** *before a Super Bowl game:*
"There will be a Monday. There will always be a Monday. But if we lose, Monday will be lousy. Tuesday will be pretty shaky too."

Brooklyn Dodger fans:
"Wait til next year."

George Allen:
"Good losers get into the habit of losing."

Southern Cal football coach **John Robinson,** *following a close win:*
"We killed them. We absolutely killed them. The only place we weren't really good was inside their two-yard line."

Dallas Cowboys general manager **Tex Schramm,** *on winning:*
"You have to look for a half of one per cent edge in as many areas as you can and that will determine if you are going to fail or succeed."

Fairleigh Dickinson basketball coach **Al LoBalbo,** *after a reporter commented that his team looked good despite losing to Seton Hall:*
"I would rather be Quasimodo and leave with Raquel Welch than be Rock Hudson and come away with Imogene Coca."

Fred Dryer *of the Los Angeles Rams, after a big win:*
"Do you know what this win feels like? It's like when a perfect woman walks into the bar at 1:55 a.m. and smiles at you."

Sign on the wall in the University of Minnesota basketball team's locker room:

"Defeat is worse than death, because you have to live with defeat."

New York Yankees owner **George Steinbrenner:**

"Winning is the greatest thing in the world, next to breathing."

New Orleans Saints coach **Bum Phillips,** *when asked if the bad weather elements had hindered his team in a 35-0 loss to Atlanta:*

"The only elements that affected us were the 11 elements wearing red jerseys."

Minnesota Vikings coach **Bud Grant:**

"There are coaches who spend 18 hours a day coaching the perfect game and they lose because the ball is oval and they have no control over the bounce."

Harold Grizzard, *football coach at Gumberry High School in North Carolina, after his team lost its 58th straight game:*

"We don't pay any attention to the scores any more. We don't even list them in the school yearbook."

Houston Rockets guard **Tom Henderson,** *explaining the club's turnaround after a slow start:*

"We started the year like hamburger but right now we're filet mignon."

Southwestern Louisiana football coach **Sam Robertson,** *when asked what he told his players when they were behind 16-0 at halftime:*

"I told them that no matter what they did in the second half I'd still love them and their mothers would still love them but I wasn't sure about their girlfriends." (USL won 40-26.)

Toronto Argonauts general manager **Lew Hayman:**

"We have to turn things around. There have been ups and downs in sports but we've been down a little longer than normal."

Montreal Canadiens forward **Dick Duff:**

"It doesn't matter if you win or lose, just don't lose."

Kevin McKenna *of the Indiana Pacers, after the club snapped its 28-game road losing streak:*

"We got together in the locker room after the game, took that monkey off our backs and beat it to death."

Lou Holtz, *on winning:*

"I can't believe God put us on this earth to be ordinary. If winning isn't important, don't keep score. Play for an hour and then quit."

Anonymous:

"Statistics are for losers."

St. Louis Cardinals manager **Whitey Herzog,** *on winning:*

"People say the toughest thing is to repeat. I think the toughest thing to do is win the first time."

Howie Long, *after his Los Angeles Raiders beat Miami 45-34:*

"It's a shame somebody had to lose but it's not a shame it was them."

Tom McLaughlin, *assistant to basketball coach Digger Phelps at Notre Dame:*

"We were 23-6 this year. Digger won 23 games and I lost six."

Pittsburgh Steelers coach **Chuck Noll:**

"I enjoy winning. If some people find that boring, we hope to bore the heck out of them."

Pittsburgh Pirates manager **Chuck Tanner:**

"I love my job. Every night I have a chance to win a major league ball game and that's the greatest thing in the world. The second greatest thing is losing a major league game because you know you're competing against the best."

Boston Celtics coach **Bill Fitch,** *after reviewing game films of a particularly bad loss:*

"Some of the things we did were so bad, so comical, that it reminded me of 'Looney Tunes.' All that tape needed at the end was Porky Pig saying: 'That's All, Folks.' "

St. Louis Cardinals pitcher **Ken Dayley,** *describing how it felt to lose the World Series:*

> "You know how it is when you have a handful of sand and it slips through your fingers? That's how we feel."

Bum Phillips:

> "A victory is like the woman you love. It may not be the absolute prettiest but it's the prettiest thing in town."

Robert Lepelletier, *explaining how he kept his cool after winning $11,702 at the racetrack:*

> "I don't have anything to spend the money on. I live next to the river. What do I need a swimming pool for?"

Toronto Argonauts coach **Leo Cahill,** *after a 30-0 loss to the B.C. Lions:*

> "We just couldn't get good field position."

Football coach, after a lop-sided loss, commenting on the other team:

> "Gee, they kickoff a lot."

Notre Dame football coach **Knute Rockne:**

> "One loss is good for the soul. Too many losses are not good for the coach."

Wake Forest football coach **Al Groh,** *after his team lost 82-24 to Clemson:*

> "I'm just glad to be alive."

Toronto Argonauts coach **Forrest Gregg,** *following a 42-3 loss to the Hamilton Tiger-Cats:*

> "The turning point in the game was when we showed up."

High school football coach **Bob James,** *after his team lost 80-0:*

> "We didn't pay any attention to the score. We had a really good time out there."

Lou Holtz, *after a loss which left the club's record at 4-3:*

> "If this is supposed to be a rebuilding year, we need urban renewal."

Billy Martin:

"If there's such a thing as a good loser, why do we bother to keep score?"

New England Patriots coach **Ron Meyer,** *describing how he felt following a particular victory:*

"No one is happier with this win than myself and my mortgage banker."

Milwaukee Bucks coach **Don Nelson,** *after a sloppy victory:*

"We don't care how the grapes are crushed, as long as the wine turns out fine."

University of Minnesota football coach **Joe Salem,** *while sitting in the interview room after a 25-7 loss to Wisconsin:*

"If you've got electricity in this chair, turn on the current."

Baylor football coach **Grant Teaff,** *after his club committed nine turnovers in a 28-23 loss to Texas A&M:*

"I feel like the federal government. That was the biggest giveaway program I've ever laid eyes on."

Wisconsin-Oshkosh basketball coach **Bob White,** *on his team's defence after an 82-58 loss:*

"You could have locked us in a phone booth with Raquel Welch and we wouldn't have gotten our hands on anything."

Freshman quarterback, after his team lost 68-0:

"Really, they weren't as good as I thought they'd be."

Maine basketball coach **Peter Gavett,** *after a 115-57 loss to Virginia:*

"I think the whole game hinged on one call, the one I made last April to schedule it."

Former NHL goaltender **Ken 'Tubby' McAuley,** *reminiscing about a game in which he gave up all 15 goals as the New York Rangers lost 15-0 to Detroit:*

"The Red Wings outplayed us so badly that the goal judge gave me the red goal light as a memento."

Cincinnati Bengals **Anthony Munoz,** *following a lop-sided loss:*

"We just got our booties blown off."

BOBBY CLARKE, AFTER HIS PHILADELPHIA FLYERS WON THE STANLEY CUP:

"NOBODY SAID WE'D WIN THE CUP, BUT WE PROVED THEM ALL WRONG."

New Orleans Saints linebacker **Rickey Jackson,** *describing his team's play after a bad game:*

"We looked like a team that had a flat tire on the side of the road and no spare."

San Francisco 49ers **Randy Cross,** *after a bad loss:*

"I don't know what happened. I was too busy having the worst game of my life."

Cedric Maxwell *of the Boston Celtics, after his team beat an opponent by more than 40 points:*

"You don't like to win by so much because it looks like you're rubbing it in. But the rules say you have to shoot every 24 seconds."

Washington Redskins **Curtis Jordan,** *after his team beat Buffalo 41-14:*

"It was close until the kickoff."

Harvard basketball player **Ken Plutnicki,** *after a disappointing loss:*

"It's like climbing the highest mountain and finding that the guru at the top doesn't know the meaning of life."

Eastern Michigan football coach **Bob Lapointe,** *after fans tore down the goal posts after his club ended a long losing streak:*

"There goes the recruiting budget but who cares."

San Antonio manager **Ducky LeJohn,** *after his team was one-hit by an opposing pitcher:*

"You can't win many games when your biggest offensive weapon is a base on balls."

Tampa Bay Buccaneers coach **John McKay,** *when asked after a bad loss what he thought of his team's execution:*

"I'm all in favor of it."

Florida football coach **Charlie Pell,** *after his team beat Georgia Tech 45-12 to boost its record to 2-0:*

"I want all the Florida folks to drive home safely because they're not used to being on the highway a winner."

Dallas Cowboys running back **Duane Thomas,** *when asked how he felt following a victory in the Super Bowl:*

"Pretty good, are they going to do this again next year?"

Cleveland Cavaliers forward **Scott Wedman,** *reflecting on a 129-79 loss to Portland:*

"When we were down by 59 points, I remember thinking that even if we scored 29 consecutive baskets, we'd still be behind. How's that for a depressing thought?"

Dallas Cowboys quarterback **Danny White,** *trying to explain how he felt during a hard-fought game with Washington:*

"It was like having a 300-pound wrestler on top of you. All you're trying to do is hang on until the end of the period."

Michigan State football coach **Muddy Waters,** *talking about the effect of an easy 61-14 game on his team:*

"It's like running the hurdles and all of a sudden you have one that's only six inches high. It throws your stride off."

University of Nebraska football coach **Tom Osborne,** *when asked if he were losing any sleep over his Cornhuskers' 31-30 loss to Miami in the national championship game:*

"I sleep like a baby. I sleep for an hour and then wake up and cry for an hour."

Basketball coach **Abe Lemons,** *after his team lost its 17th game:*

"I'd rather be a football coach. That way, you can only lose 11 games."

Brown University coach **Jon Anderson,** *after his team lost to highly-favored Penn State by a respectable score of 38-21:*

"Someone told me this game would be like Custer's last stand but we had a much better game plan than Custer."

Houston Oilers coach **Bum Phillips,** *after his team beat New England 38-34:*

"Our prevent defence almost prevented us from winning."

CHAPTER 20

PHYSICAL MAKE-UP

"He looks like the 15th green at Pebble Beach."

Former major league slugger **Al Oliver** always maintained that a batter should be able to hit his weight. He insisted if a batter could not hit his weight, he should not be in the line-up. That theory almost resulted in heavy embarrassment.

Oliver was with the Montreal Expos at the time and was struggling at the plate.

"I weigh 205 pounds and I went into the game hitting an even .200, so the pressure was on," he explained. "If I had gone 0-for-4, I would have put myself on a diet."

Luckily, Oliver had three hits in the game to move his batting average higher than his weight.

Tom Paciorek *of the Chicago White Sox, talking about the strength of teammate Ron Kittle:*

"The last guy I saw as strong as Kittle was hanging from the Empire State Building and had Fay Wray in his arms."

University of Colorado football coach **Bill McCartney,** *describing one of his defensive backs:*

"He's the kind of kid you like to have in there because he foams at the mouth and chases cars."

Former Washington Redskins quarterback **Sonny Jurgenson,** *on his lack of speed:*

"The TV people broke for a commercial as I started a 33-yard touchdown run. They came back and I was still running."

Los Angeles Dodgers manager **Tommy Lasorda:**

"Giving up linguine should be classified as un-American."

Louisiana State running back **Hokie Gajan,** *talking about his speed:*

"The only time I have breakaway speed is when the other team has defensive linemen playing the deep secondary."

Buffalo Bills centre **Mark Traynowicz,** *talking about his crew cut hair style:*

"Believe it or not, where I come from (Nebraska), I'm good-looking."

Baltimore Orioles pitcher **Tippy Martinez,** *after he learned the club had traded 300-pound reliever Tim Stoddard to Oakland:*

"Good. Now, after the games, there'll be more food on the table for everybody."

Sportswriter **Frank Orr,** *about Pittsburgh Penguins goaltender Denis Herron:*

"He's so skinny he could hide behind a goal post."

Baseball great **Ted Williams,** *long after his retirement, when a security guard failed to recognize him at a charity event:*

"I know I'm old, fat, and ugly but I'm still Ted Williams."

New York Yankees infielder **Roy Smalley,** *on the teasing he receives from teammates about his designer wardrobe:*

"They get on me but they all dress like Walt Garrison and think Giorgio Armani plays for the New York Cosmos."

Los Angeles Lakers centre **Kareem Abdul-Jabbar,** *on what it's like to be 7'2":*

"I've always identified with the California redwoods and the Empire State Building."

Lineman **Norm Evans,** *as he announced his retirement from the Seattle Seahawks:*

"I'm going to quit while I'm still healthy. I'm the only guy I know who has been around the NFL for 14 years and doesn't have zippers on his knees."

Detroit Tigers outfielder **Champ Summers,** *commenting on a spell of muggy weather:*

"I've already spent $3,500 on deodorant."

Pitcher **Bill Lee,** *on slugger Cliff Johnson:*

"As long as he keeps those little slits for eyes, a manager will never look in to see if he's gone."

Texas Rangers outfielder **Mickey Rivers:**

"The ugliest player I ever saw was Danny Napoleon. He was so ugly that when you walked by, your clothes would wrinkle."

Basketball commentator **Eddie Doucette:**

"Houston forward Joe Bryant has become so fat that he could set a double pick all by himself."

New Orleans Saints safety **Bobby Johnson,** *trying to describe the feeling he gets when he tackles Chicago's Walter Payton:*

"The only thing I can compare it to is when I was little and playing football. I ran into a tree."

6'11" **Darryl Dawkins,** *talking about the tiny hotel rooms he stayed in during a trip to Israel and Italy:*

"I could do everything from my bed. I could answer the door, answer the phone, turn on the television and go to the bathroom. And when I rolled over, I elbowed somebody on the elevator."

Washington Redskins running back **John Riggins,** *on some nagging injuries:*

"That's the trouble with a make and model my age, it's hard to get parts."

Chicago Bears defensive lineman **Dan Hampton,** *who had surgery on his right knee and then returned to the line-up only to suffer an injury to his left knee:*

"In an instant, my bad knee became my good knee."

Sportscaster **Skip Caray,** *explaining how short Kansas City Kings coach Cotton Fitzsimmons is:*

"He's the only coach in the NBA who can sleep in a pillowcase."

Texas Christian University football coach **F. A. Dry,** *after his scouts came back from the University of Southern California:*

"They tell me some of the USC linemen can stand flat-footed and see Denver."

Vanderbilt football coach **George MacIntyre,** *after he heard that Georgia running back Herschel Walker had been injured in practice:*

"Herschel Walker scares me. But what scares me even more is knowing that Georgia has players tough enough to hurt him."

Minnesota Vikings coach **Bud Grant,** *on the physical problems of older players:*

"Any player over 30 in this league has something bad, likely bad enough to get a 40-per cent disability in this state."

Chicago Bulls broadcaster **Jim Durham,** *talking about a 6'11" player:*

"If you went to the movies with him, they'd let you in for half-price."

New England Patriots coach **Ron Meyer,** *on the team's search for players following a series of injuries:*

"We don't know if our newest player is any good or not. All we know is that he's got a heartbeat and we found him walking down the street."

Miami Dolphins running back **Larry Csonka:**

"It's good to have linemen you can look straight in the belly button."

Philadelphia 76ers general manager **Pat Williams,** *on 275-pound forward Charles Barkley:*

"Charles is so fat he once fell down and rocked himself to sleep trying to get up."

Murray State football coach **Mike Gottfried,** *talking about a 6'6", 410-pound lineman:*

"He creates a real problem at practice. The guys playing next to him are always looking out of the corner of their eyes to see which way he's going to fall. They're afraid of getting buried."

University of Mississippi tackle **Lawrence Johnson,** *talking about his flat feet:*

"I can kill a bug from any angle."

Miami Dolphins quarterback **Bob Griese,** *pinpointing when the criticism of his lack of height stopped:*

"When I won two Super Bowls."

Football coach, on a 334-pound lineman:

"We have him on a lettuce diet. He's now eating 40 pounds of lettuce a day."

Gordie Howe, *talking about Bobby Hull who spent the off-season on his cattle ranch:*

"He's so strong he doesn't call the cattle in, he carries them in."

Baltimore Orioles pitcher **Jim Palmer,** *when asked what it would take for the New York Yankees to sign Earl Weaver as manager:*

"As soon as somebody tells him he'll look taller in pinstripes, he'll sign the contract."

Darryl Dawkins, *talking about the beard on one of his teammates:*

"You could take that thing and make a heckuva pot scrubber out of it."

Stanford football coach **Tom Lovat,** *when asked why most of the team's running backs were under six feet tall:*

"Because our line can only make holes six feet high."

Sportscaster **Jay Randolph,** *describing Pittsburgh Pirates pitcher Kent Tekulve:*

"He's as thin as the centre field foul pole."

Philadelphia Flyers goaltender **Pete Peeters:**

"I don't know why Wayne Gretzky got those jean commercials ahead of me. I've got a prettier bum than he has."

Sportscaster **Tom Brookshier,** *talking about Atlanta tight end Junior Miller,who stands 6'4" and weighs 243 pounds:*

"If he's Junior Miller, I'd hate to see Senior Miller."

Sportswriter **Bernie Linicome:**

"White Sox pitcher LaMarr Hoyt looks like a baker in love with his own buns. You figure the only way he could make a living in baseball is to be paid by the pound."

Los Angeles Lakers broadcaster **Chick Hearn,** *describing slender Michael Cooper:*

"They have to put plugs in the drains when he takes a shower."

Tommy Lasorda, *on his waistline:*

"When we were playing well, I was happy and ate a lot. When we were playing lousy, I got nervous and ate a lot."

St. Louis Cardinals lineman **Dan Dierdorf,** *on his retirement:*

"Ninety-five per cent of me is very sad that I'm retiring. But my knees are very, very happy."

Commentator **Bucky Waters,** *talking about 5'5" Kentucky guard Leroy Byrd:*

"He's a great addition to your bench. He can sit on it or under it."

Noel Cantwell, *coach of the Jacksonville Tea Men of the North American Soccer League, describing the complexion of a new recruit from England:*

"He looks like a milk bottle."

Bud Harrelson *of the New York Mets, on 6'7", 300-pound Frank Howard:*

"Singe him a little and the Argentine army could feed off him for a year."

Delaware University centre **Tim Carr,** *when he was asked about being 6'11":*

"The weather up here is clear and sunny with plenty of rebounds in the future."

Oakland Raiders defensive end **John Matuszak,** *on the main difference between the Raiders and their Super Bowl opponents, the Philadelphia Eagles:*

"We're cuter."

230

Golfer **Billy Casper,** *on his physical condition:*

"Like a lot of fellows my age, I have a furniture problem. My chest has fallen into my drawers."

Cincinnati Reds relief pitcher **Brad Lesley,** *who stands 6'6" and weighs 240 pounds:*

"On my first trip to New York I decided to check out the subway. It was beautiful and everybody was so nice to me. Of course, who's going to mug a guy like me when there are so many little old ladies around?"

Ed Croke *of the New York Giants, on 295-pound defensive end Leonard Marshall:*

"We put him on a Cambridge diet and he ate half of Cambridge."

Bobby Valentine *of the Chicago Cubs, talking about hefty catcher Barry Foote:*

"There's one guy who spends all his meal money. None of it gets mailed home."

University of Arizona quarterback **Tom Tunnicliffe:**

"Any NFL coach who feels I'm too short to play is too stupid for me to play for anyway."

Moses Malone *of the Philadelphia 76ers, when asked if he took drugs:*

"I'm 6'10". That's high enough."

Green Bay Packers defensive end **Ezra Johnson,** *who was fined $1,000 for eating a hot dog on the sidelines during an exhibition game:*

"It would have been different if I had eaten the thing because we were losing or because of disrespect. But I ate it because I was hungry."

Portland Trail Blazers forward **Mychal Thompson,** *talking about 7'7" Manute Bol of Washington:*

"I don't know why NASA spends all that money on the space shuttle. All they've got to do is give Manute some tools and let him reach up and fix things."

An anonymous teammate, about Seattle SuperSonics forward Lonnie Shelton:
"When we go on the road and Lonnie puts on his green uniform, he looks like the 15th green at Pebble Beach."

Doug English *of the Detroit Lions, on Cleveland Browns centre Mike Baab:*
"Mike Baab is as strong as nine acres of Texas onions."

High school athletic director **Jim McClune,** *talking about a football player who stands 6'6" and weighs 345 pounds:*
"His shoulder pads look like the bumpers on a Mack truck."

Darryl Dawkins, *on a particularly tall opponent:*
"He's so tall that if he fell down, he'd be halfway home."

CFL commissioner **Jake Gaudaur,** *talking about a player with big feet:*
"He's the only guy I know who has to put his pants on over his head."

CFL executive **Herb Capozzi,** *about former player Vince Mazza:*
"Mazza was told one must have a healthy body and a sound mind. He thought he had to make a choice."

Oral Roberts University centre **Tom Prusator,** *addressing a media luncheon:*
"This speech won't take long. I thought when I came here that all I'd have to do is eat."

New York Islanders forward **Mike Bossy,** *after a reporter suggested that his hair was turning grey:*
"That's a pigment of your imagination."

Sportswriter, describing an overweight George Chuvalo:
"Not only did he have a pot belly, he also had a pot back."

Basketball commentator **Bucky Waters,** *about a 275-pound player:*
"His thighs could go condo."

WILLIAM PERRY:
"I WAS BIG WHEN I WAS LITTLE."

Kansas City Royals trainer **Mickey Cobb,** *on his first visit to Montreal:*

"I didn't have any trouble ordering at restaurants. French toast for breakfast. French onion soup for lunch. French dip for dinner."

Kareem Abdul-Jabbar, *on his height problems as a child:*

"My mother used to send me to the movies with my birth certificate so I wouldn't have to pay the extra 50 cents for the adult admission."

New York Yankees coach **Gene Michael,** *after he quit smoking:*

"I'm going to be awfully mad if they find out 10 years from now that smoking is good for you."

Carlton Fisk, *beginning a new career as a left fielder, after watching a home run go into the stands:*

"For some hitters, I'll have to learn to play taller."

Philadelphia 76ers general manager **Pat Williams,** *talking about a particularly slender player:*

"He's so skinny his pajamas have only one pinstripe."

Miami Dolphins fullback **Larry Csonka,** *after a good game:*

"The holes might not have been big enough to drive a truck through but they were big enough for a fat old fullback."

Darryl Dawkins, *when asked if he had grown more mature since beginning his pro career:*

"I don't think so. I think I'm about as grown as I'm going to get."

Baltimore Orioles pitcher **Jim Palmer,** *after manager Earl Weaver held a closed-door meeting with his team:*

"He was swearing at everyone and leaping up and down. I've never seen him so tall."

North Carolina State centre **Chuck Nevitt,** *on being 7'5":*

"My father is 6'7" and my mother is six-foot. At least I've never worried if I was adopted."

Former hockey player and entertainer **Eddie Shack:**

"I've got a nose for value."

Al Oliver, *after he reported to training camp a little overweight and was taken to task by team management:*

"Ain't no fat on my bat."

North Carolina basketball coach **Dean Smith,** *on a new rule that high school students must have at least a 'C' average to be eligible for college sport:*

"Everyone has a 'C' average if he's over 6'6"."

Baltimore Orioles pitcher **Don Stanhouse:**

"Doctors once X-rayed my hair and they found flowers."

Atlanta Braves manager **Joe Torre,** *talking about his thinning hair:*

"I've gone to the Watergate hairdo. I cover up everything I can."

University of Oklahoma defensive line coach **Rex Norris,** *describing Nebraska's offensive team:*

"Watching Nebraska break the huddle is like watching six refrigerators roll down a hill."

Bill Veeck, *talking about midget Eddie Gaedel whom he once sent up to pinch-hit:*

"He'd have been great in a short series."

U.S. Olympic hockey coach **Lou Vairo,** *talking about when he weighed 256 pounds:*

"I'd get on the scales and a card would come down: 'One at a time, please.' "

Canisius College football coach **Tom Hershey,** *commenting on 5'4" running back Mike Panepinto:*

"He's the only running back I know of who has to jump up to take a handoff."

Milwaukee Bucks assistant coach **John Killilea,** *talking about an extremely muscular opponent:*

"He looks like he worked on the Nautilus all summer. Either that, or he carried the machines in every day."

Mickey Rivers, *on teammate Cliff Johnson:*

"He's so ugly we should put an oxygen mask on him."

Art Donovan, *a 300-pound Baltimore Colts lineman, describing himself as a light eater:*

"As soon as it's light, I start eating."

Houston Astros executive assistant **Donald Davidson,** *on why the team hired Yogi Berra as a coach:*

"We need somebody at spring training to scare away the alligators."

New York Giants linebacker **Casey Merrill,** *after he settled his contract dispute:*

"I'm glad to be back in New York. Where else can you have bagels for breakfast, soul food for lunch and tacos for dinner?"

Auburn basketball coach **Sonny Smith,** *explaining how he encouraged an overweight athlete to slim down:*

"I told him: 'If it tastes good, spit it out.' "

Houston Oilers general manager **Ladd Herzeg,** *talking about a prospect whose career ended when he ballooned to 330 pounds:*

"We thought he would be all-Pro. He turned out to be all-Cafeteria."

Tommy Lasorda, *on what it would take to get some secret information out of him:*

"Buy me a dinner and you'll loosen my tongue. Linguine is a mind-altering substance."

CHAPTER 21

BRUTALLY HONEST

"The guy who stole my suede coat."

Even as a youngster, **Bobby Fischer** was an aggressive chess player. He was also so good at the game at such a young age that he often had to play both ends of the board to give himself a challenge.

"I tried to be fair and play the best moves for both sides," he recalls. "But I usually won."

Willie Mays:

"I thought I was the best player I ever saw. When I played pro ball, I felt that nobody in the world could do what I could do on a baseball field."

New Orleans Saints coach **Bum Phillips,** *to Johnny Carson on the Tonight show:*

"I usually take my wife with me on road trips because she's too ugly to kiss goodbye."

Tampa Bay Buccaneers running back **Jerry Eckwood,** *explaining that his wife was studying mortuary science:*

"She's the one who puts the happy face on you when it's all over."

Sportswriter **Art Spander:**

"San Francisco's Candlestick Park is a great place if you like pneumonia, misplayed fly balls and swirling hot-dog wrappers."

Anne Hayes, *when asked if she had ever considered divorcing her husband, Ohio State coach Woody Hayes:*

"Divorce, no. Murder, yes."

Placekicker **Rich Karlis,** *explaining why he reported early to the Denver Broncos training camp:*

"I'm not married and I don't have anybody to cook for me. No more hamburgers for at least four weeks."

Steve Garvey, *on Pete Rose:*

"When they asked God to make a baseball player, He carved out Pete Rose. The rest of us were made from chips off the mold."

Atlanta Falcons defensive end **Jeff Merrow,** *explaining why he doesn't like Monday night games:*

"The late start doesn't give us much time to hit the bars afterward."

Columnist **Mike Lupica,** *talking about Washington Redskins quarterback Joe Theismann:*

"If talking were an Olympic sport, Theismann would be Jim Thorpe."

Unknown cab driver, after he was told the hapless Brooklyn Dodgers had three men on base:

"Which base?"

Sportswriter **Blackie Sherrod:**

"When Darrell Royal refers to his Texas Longhorns as student athletes, it's like calling the postmen 'gentlemen of dedicated delivery.' "

Green Bay Packers coach **Forrest Gregg,** *when asked if he were worried about the morale of his 1-7 team:*

"They better worry about mine."

Sportswriter **Glenn Schwarz,** *after Milwaukee blasted Oakland 11-3 on Jacket Day at the park:*

"Instead of handing out jackets, the A's should have passed out blindfolds."

Toronto Argonauts coach **Leo Cahill,** *when asked by the club owner whether he was going to the Grey Cup:*

"I know I am but I don't know about our team."

Tampa Bay coach **John McKay,** *talking about taking his 0-8 Buccaneers on a three-game road trip:*

> "It will be good for us to go on the road. I think the home fans have seen enough of us."

San Diego Padres pitcher **Chris Welsh,** *explaining that he regretted an incident in which he defied manager Dick Williams:*

> "I'm just not good enough to be a jerk and get away with it."

Football coach **Lou Holtz,** *commenting on his formal education:*

> "I'm not really very smart. I went to school primarily to eat my lunch."

Football coach:

> "I don't know why people question the academic training of a student athlete. Half the doctors in the country graduated in the bottom half of their class."

Joe DiMaggio, *when asked to comment on the reference to him in the Simon and Garfunkle song Mrs. Robinson:*

> "I've never been able to figure out what that song means."

Sportswriter **Dick Young,** *when someone pointed out that the NFL players' strike had actually decreased drug abuse in the league:*

> "Without a paycheque, who could afford the stuff?"

Bobby Bonds, *as a member of the Cleveland Indians:*

> "The only good thing about playing in Cleveland is that you don't have to go there on road trips."

Republican **Jack Kemp,** *on the difference between football and politics:*

> "In football, the enemies have numbers on and are always out front where you can see them. That's not always the case in politics."

Detroit Tigers infielder **Dave Bergman,** *talking about the club's demanding schedule:*

> "The guys who made up this schedule must have been in a room with a bottle of Wild Turkey and 40 straws."

Chicago White Sox slugger **Ron Kittle:**
"My parents never saw me play when I was with Edmonton. It takes two donkeys and a ski boat to get there."

Cleveland Browns running back **Jimmy Brown,** *when asked why he walked so slowly back to the huddle:*
"They don't pay me to run back to the huddle."

University of Texas football coach **Fred Akers,** *on his approach to academics:*
"Not all of my players are geniuses but they're sure going to study or they won't be players."

Sportswriter **Red Smith:**
"The only people who think baseball is dull are those people with dull minds."

Oscar Homolka:
"Baseball may be the national pastime in America but surely dieting is a close second."

Soviet leader **Nikita Krushchev,** *about U.S. football:*
"They all stand up, they all fall down, it's a stupid game."

Agent **George Andrews,** *after he was told that advice columnist Ann Landers had attended a Chicago Bulls game:*
"If Ann Landers was at a Bulls game, she has a problem."

Bum Phillips, *when asked if he had ever played college football:*
"I thought I did until I looked at some old game films."

Prime Minister **Pierre Trudeau,** *during a tough time for the Toronto Argonauts:*
"Perhaps we should make the Argos a crown corporation. Even if we could run them as efficiently as the Post Office, it would still be an improvement."

Bill Lee, *after his trade from Boston:*
"I'm glad to be leaving the Red Sox. I hated to be associated with a team that will go down in history with the '64 Phillies and the '67 Arabs."

Sportswriter **Art Spander,** *on how quickly the skills and fame of great athletes can fade:*

"Yesterday's hero is today's waiver listee."

Sportswriter **Dave Daley:**

"There is no off-season in Chicago. It's only when the teams start playing that the fans lose interest."

Al McGuire, *as chairman of the President's council on physical fitness, suggesting a motto:*

"Okay, everyone up and off their duff."

H. L. Mencken:

"I hate all sports as rabidly as a person who likes sports hates common sense."

William Shakespeare:

"If all the year were playing holidays, to sport would be as tedious as to work."

Sports fan, watching television, to his wife and kids:

"All I want is a little peace and quiet during the football, hockey and baseball seasons. Is that too much to ask?"

Pittsburgh Pirates public relations director **Joe Safety,** *joking about the club's oldest employee:*

"He's older than dirt."

Toronto Argonauts guard **Joel Parrish,** *after a series of incidents involving vandalism to his van:*

"It could be a Hamilton Ti-cat fan."

Anonymous sports fan in Chicago:

"Chicago has more dog teams than the Yukon."

Dodgertown chef **Jesse Crawford,** *when asked the difference between feeding the Los Angeles Dodgers baseball players and the New Orleans Saints football players:*

"About two steaks per player."

Anonymous:

"We all love a good loser, if it isn't us."

Seattle SuperSonics owner **Sam Schulman,** *on his team's success:*

"It's a miracle and I deserve to have it happen to me."

Diana Backstrom, *the young daughter of hockey star Ralph Backstrom, after he told her that he was going to a hockey school:*

"Are you going to teach or learn?"

Bob Hope:

"I've watched so much football lately, I've worn out my end zone."

Tilbury mayor **Joe Young,** *explaining why the local arena was always full despite the fact the Tilbury Bluebirds had lost 43 straight games:*

"Nobody wants to miss it in case we ever win one."

Air Force football coach **Ben Martin:**

"Our team flies United. I don't trust those Air Force planes."

Tiger Lyons *of Chicago, talking about attendance at USFL games:*

"The way it's going, the 'final four' could be the crowd at the next Blitz game."

Mickey Mantle, *on the relationship between Billy Martin and George Steinbrenner:*

"If Billy goes undefeated, they'll get along fine."

Football fan in New Jersey, when asked if the New York Giants should change their name to the New Jersey Giants because they play their home games at East Rutherford, N.J.:

"No. New Jersey doesn't need the humiliation of calling the Giants their own."

Indiana football coach **Lee Corso,** *explaining how he gets along with the school's basketball coach, Bobby Knight:*

"Very well. I just do everything he tells me."

Former NBA player and coach **Tommy Heinsohn,** *talking about the playoffs:*

"They go on and on, like a guy telling a bad joke for 15 minutes."

Soccer player **Clive Charles,** *when asked whom he would most like to meet in the whole world:*

"The guy who stole my suede coat."

Ron Kittle, *when asked why he prefers to wear glasses over contact lenses:*

"I was never too crazy about putting my fingers in my eyeballs."

Baseball commissioner **Kenesaw Mountain Landis,** *after the infamous 'Black Sox' scandal of 1919:*

"Regardless of the verdict of juries, no player that throws a ball game, no player that undertakes or promises to throw a ball game, no player that sits in conference with a bunch of crooked players and gamblers where the ways and means of throwing games are planned and discussed and does not promptly tell his club about it, will ever play professional baseball."

Dick Beddoes:

"The sportswriting fraternity is burdened with hacks who make tin-can Gods out of cast-iron jerks."

Fred Schwartz, *the director of a croquet tournament in Washington, D.C.:*

"The only qualification for this game is that a player have absolutely no sense of remorse. Politicians make good croquet players."

Anonymous baseball fan in Chicago:

"There's a transit crisis here. People are worried they might get on a bus to Wrigley Field and get stuck there."

Sportscaster **Bob Miller,** *after thieves broke into the Los Angeles Kings' dressing room:*

"I bet they didn't get any Stanley Cup rings."

Sportscaster **Merlin Olsen,** *talking about San Francisco defensive end Fred Dean:*

"There aren't enough expletives in the book to describe Fred Dean."

Sportswriter **Bill Conlin,** *on the speed of Pete Rose:*

"Bulk-rate mail beats him down the line."

Prime Minister **Pierre Trudeau:**

"Canada's main exports are hockey players and cold fronts. Our main imports are baseball players and acid rain."

Bum Phillips, *addressing the rookie camp:*

"If you think you can get up at 6 a.m., work out twice a day, stay on the field five hours, go to meetings and then party all night and still have a chance to make this team, more power to you."

Sportscaster **Bill Good Jr.,** *after a bad game by the Vancouver Canucks:*

"If the Canucks had played in your backyard Saturday night, you would have closed the drapes."

Sportswriter **Dave Distel,** *after the San Diego Padres announced they were moving their outfield fences in to take advantage of their power hitters:*

"The Padres moving their fences in is like re-arranging the deck chairs on the Titanic."

Cleveland Indians third baseman **Toby Harrah,** *during a poor season:*

"If we work really hard, we might be able to get back to mediocrity."

Dallas Cowboys tight end **Doug Cosbie,** *when asked what he would do if he ever owned the team:*

"I would raise the price and re-sell. I wouldn't want to put up with all the players and their salary demands."

Terry Kennedy *of the San Diego Padres, talking about the club's inconsistency:*

"One day we play like King Kong, the next day we play like Fay Wray."

University of Michigan basketball coach **Bill Frieder,** *talking about his team's chances of beating Illinois and Purdue on the road:*

"I'd have a better chance of finding Jimmy Hoffa."

Calgary Flames defenceman **Brad Marsh,** *at a sports banquet where roast beef was served:*

"I always liked roast beef, until tonight."

New York Yankees third baseman **Graig Nettles,** *during a particularly controversial season:*

"When I was growing up, I wanted to either run away and join the circus, or play major league baseball. I was lucky. Here in New York, I got to do both."

Basketball observer, summing up the playoff performance of Los Angeles Lakers forward Kurt Rambis:

"Rambis looked like Clark Kent, rebounded like Superman and shot like Lois Lane."

George Blanda, *when asked why he thought some of his NFL records would never be broken:*

"Because no one is stupid enough to play 26 years any more."

Dean Dickey:

"If you want to lose weight, eat three meals a day, snack between meals and eat anything you want and as much as you want — but only on days after the Chicago Cubs win."

Sportswriter **Tony Kornheiser:**

"How bad are the Philadelphia Eagles? They are worse than inept. They are even worse than unept. They are so far away from ept it's a toll call."

Sportswriter **John Herbert,** *about the marketing director of a particular hockey team:*

"He couldn't market a gold brick."

Sportswriter **Dave Overpeck,** *on the Chicago Bulls:*

"The Bulls are the bar girls of the NBA — they promise a lot but deliver little."

Darryl Sittler, *after his trade from Philadelphia to Detroit:*
"It's a cold-hearted business. There are no loyalties."

Heavyweight boxer **Mike Tyson,** *outlining his strategy:*
"Well, I always try to drive my fist into the tip of the nose, pushing the nose bone into the brain. After that, I know they don't want it any more."

Former Montreal Canadiens defenceman **Doug Harvey,** *when asked if he were a better defenceman than Bobby Orr or Paul Coffey:*
"I don't know. I never saw myself play."

Dayton University basketball coach **Don Donoher:**
"I feel athletics are for participants. Coaches are just a necessary evil."

A pro hockey player, who preferred to remain anonymous:
"Hockey is going to degenerate further if we don't start chasing the puck instead of the buck."

Pete Rose:
"I'm the type of guy fathers want their sons to grow up to be but wouldn't want their daughters to go out with."

Louisiana State basketball coach **Dale Brown,** *after a dismal effort by his team:*
"We're not the LSU Tigers, we're the LSU Somnambulists. When we're the Tigers again, I'll let you know."

Pitcher **Chris Welsh,** *after being cut by the Texas Rangers:*
"It's a blow to your ego to get released by the worst team in the universe."

Comedian **Bill Cosby,** *during his induction into Temple University's Hall of Fame:*
"I now feel I can represent all mediocrity."

Chicago sportswriter **Mike Royko,** *when asked what he thought of the NFL players' strike:*
"You should really ask that of someone from a city that has a pro football team."

Anders Kallur *of the New York Islanders, when asked why the national hockey team of his native Sweden was doing poorly in world competition:*

"Too many Swedes. One or two is okay but 20 is too many."

John Matuszak *of the Oakland Raiders, after someone suggested that he stop going into bars:*

"I'll stay out of bars when the women promise not to go in them."

Frank Robinson, *on his career:*

"People ask me if I'm sorry I didn't get 3,000 hits and 600 home runs. I don't think I have to apologize for getting 2,943 hits and 586 homers."

San Diego Padres manager **Dick Williams,** *on his working relationship with general manager Jack McKeon:*

"Jack and I get along well because he's as easy-going as I am obnoxious."

Bum Phillips, *in response to players who say they use drugs for recreation:*

"That's like saying you rob banks for fun."

Sportswriter **Art Spander:**

"Candlestick Park is the only baseball park in which you start the day putting on Coppertone and end it by putting on a parka."

CHAPTER 22

COME AGAIN? SAY WHAT?

"Our similarities are different."

During the 7 1/2 years I hosted a sports talk show on radio, kids continually contributed. One call from a youngster stands out in my mind and likely always will. He was about 11 or 12 years old and called about a baseball question. Imagine, if you possibly can, this conversation on your radio.

GAP: "Sports Call, you're on the air."

KID: "Yeah, Gary, I think I've got the answer to that baseball question you asked."

GAP: "All right. Just before we hear your answer, let me review the situation for those people who may have missed it, okay?"

KID: "Okay."

GAP: "A baseball team has a runner on first base and one man out. The batter hits a sharp ground ball to the first baseman who immediately steps on first and then throws to second. You are the second base umpire, what's your call?"

KID: "I call the runner out but only if he's tagged because there's no longer a force play at second."

GAP: "How do you figure that?"

KID: "Well, if the ball goes to second first and first second, then it's a force play. But if the ball goes to first first and second second, then it's not."

GAP: "Let me make sure I understand what you're saying here. If the ball goes to first first and second second as opposed to first second and second first, there has to be a tag, right?"

KID: (pause) "I'm not sure about that. (another pause) If the ball goes first to second and second to first, it's a force play. But if the ball goes first to first and second to second, it's not."

GAP: "How can a ball go first to first? And if the ball goes first to second, it would have to go to first first, wouldn't it?"

KID: (pause) "Uh, I guess so."

GAP: "So if the ball goes to first first, it would have to go first to second second, not second to first second. Of course, if the ball goes to second first, it would go second to first second instead of first to second second and that would be a force play, right?"

KID: (pause) "I think so."

GAP: "Okay, you explain it one final time so everyone has it."

KID: (long pause) "If the ball goes to second first and....no.... yeah, that's right. If the ball goes to second first and first second, it's a force play. But if the ball goes to first first and second second, there has to be a tag on the runner."

GAP: "Perfect! Well done! Sounds like you should be an umpire."

KID: "Yeah, but after this call, I think I'd rather work at third."

Yogi Berra, *after Johnny Bench passed him on the all-time list of home run-hitting catchers:*
"Yeah, but he hit all his on artificial turf."

A sports reporter, after Tennessee beat USC 91-90 in overtime:
"The game was closer than the score would indicate."

Former Hamilton Tiger-Cat **Vince Mazza,** *defending a trade the club had made:*
"Look, I been there and I'll tell you it only takes one bad apple to spoil the rest of the fruits."

Charlie Waters *of the Dallas Cowboys, after viewing a computerized creation of a game between the Cowboys and some all-time greats:*

> "For an 84-year-old Indian, Jim Thorpe showed me some great moves."

Baltimore Orioles manager **Earl Weaver,** *on the overall strength of his team:*

> "We've got deep depth."

Los Angeles Raiders linebacker **Matt Millen:**

> "We have a dress code for the plane. You can't look like a pig."

University of Minnesota coach **Joe Salem,** *when asked if his team was the victim of Murphy's Law during a losing streak:*

> "No, Murphy has been one of our better players."

Former major league manager **John McGraw,** *to one of his players:*

> "You have more talent per square head than anyone else in the league."

San Francisco 49ers coach **Bill Walsh,** *when asked if one of his players would be fined for missing a practice because of an upset stomach:*

> "It's an internal matter."

Toronto Argonauts coach **Willie Wood,** *after another frustrating loss:*

> "We have to work out our crooks and nannies."

Texas Rangers outfielder **Mickey Rivers:**

> "My goals for this year are to hit .300, score 100 runs and stay injury-prone."

Brigham Young University wide receiver **Glen Kozlowski,** *explaining his school's strict code of conduct:*

> "We can't drink, we can't smoke and we can't chase women. Well, we can chase women but we aren't allowed to catch them."

COME AGAIN? SAY WHAT?

Yogi Berra, *on attendance problems:*

"If people don't want to come out to the park, nobody's going to stop 'em."

Arkansas football coach **Lou Holtz,** *when asked what he would like written on his tombstone:*

" 'To my wife, I told you I was sick.' "

Football coach, when asked if he had enjoyed his honeymoon:

"I won't know until I see the films."

Terry McGuire, *wife of NBA scout Dick McGuire, on her knowledge of the game;*

"To win, you've got to put the ball in the macrame."

Anne Hayes, *about her husband Woody, the football coach at Ohio State:*

"A lot of people say you either love my husband or you hate his guts. That's not entirely true. In my case, I love him and I also hate his guts."

California State football coach **Jack Elway,** *when asked how he planned to recruit his own son, quarterback John Elway:*

"I've offered him free room and board, a new car and cash under the table. I also told him I'd go as far as to have an affair with his mother."

Baseball fan **Jamie Reynolds,** *after he married his fiancee at home plate prior to a Portland Beavers home game:*

"I promised her a big diamond and this was the biggest one I could find."

Sportswriter, at the 1980 Lake Placid Olympics which were plagued by transportation problems:

"There is good news and bad news. The good news is that the Soviet Union is willing to withdraw its troops from Afghanistan. The bad news is that the Lake Placid Organizing Committee has the contract to bus them out."

Atlanta Braves outfielder **Claudell Washington,** *after the Braves won their first 13 games of the season:*

"If things keep going like this, we expect to go all the way."

Bill Lee, *on the baseball players' strike:*

"I didn't vote for the strike. I voted for worse. I wanted the players to own the parks. I wanted to sell organic burgers, have rock concerts after the games and mini-marathons. I'd design the parks around the planet we live on."

Montreal Alouettes defensive lineman **Glen Weir,** *after limping off the field with a leg injury:*

"I've got a headache in my knee."

Former NFL player **Alex Hawkins,** *putting his own talent into perspective:*

"I was bad enough to play for a good team but not good enough to play for a bad team."

Yogi Berra, *to a reporter:*

"I wish I had an answer for that, because I'm tired of answering that question."

Washington Redskins running back **John Riggins,** *explaining why he needs to win another Super Bowl title:*

"My Super Bowl ring is quite heavy. To keep from walking around in circles the rest of my life, I'll need another ring the same size on the other hand."

A disgruntled Chicago Cubs fan, after the American hostages in Iran had been released:

"I know how to gain revenge on the Ayatollah. Let's give him a 444-game pass to see the Cubs."

Buffalo Bills running back **Greg Bell,** *when asked if he could fill the shoes of Joe Cribbs:*

"Joe is smaller than me and I doubt that we wear the same size."

Former Pittsburgh Steelers quarterback **Terry Bradshaw,** *during a telecast from Riverfront Stadium in Cincinnati:*

"I have a lot of fond memories from playing here and many of them are negative."

Bum Phillips, *after passing a physical:*

"If I drop dead tomorrow, at least I'll know I died in good health."

Detroit Tigers pitcher **Mark 'The Bird' Fidrych,** *on the possibility of a players' strike:*

> "If the other players strike, so will I. You can't play this game by yourself."

Tampa Bay Buccaneers defensive end **Cedric Brown,** *trying to explain his team's losing streak:*

> "Every week, 28 NFL teams play. Twelve gotta win, 12 gotta lose."

Yogi Berra, *after the Yankees played their home opener:*

> "Home openers are always exciting, whether they're at home or on the road."

University of Indiana football coach **Lee Corso:**

> "This year we've got Michigan just where we want them. We don't play them."

Peter Koech, *a distance runner from Kenya, on the training conditions in his homeland:*

> "It's a jungle out there."

Pittsburgh Steelers coach **Chuck Noll,** *explaining what happens when two football teams meet:*

> "You take the factors of your own team and put them with the factors of the other team and what you get is a geometric explosion of the factors involved."

New York Mets catcher **John Stearns,** *talking about the chances of a players' strike:*

> "I'd say there's a 99 per cent chance of a strike. The players are 110 per cent unified on this issue."

Mike Perkins, *when asked if he planned to go to the University of Alabama, the alma mater of his father, New York Giants coach Ray Perkins:*

> "No, I don't want to go there. I want to get an education."

Marathoner **Alberto Salazar,** *concerned about possible smog conditions at the Los Angeles Olympics, explaining how he might train:*

> "I might start the car in the garage and run in there."

Notre Dame coach **Knute Rockne:**

> "The result of any vote on a football team will always be seven to four."

Man, to his friend at a health club:

> "I've really been lucky. I've managed to exercise and still stay fat."

Mickey Rivers, *discussing the winds in Arlington Stadium:*

> "They must be blowing at 100 degrees."

Dale Berra, *when asked to compare himself to his father Yogi:*

> "Our similarities are different."

A young cashier in a sporting goods store, holding up a pair of catcher's shin guards:

> "Are these $29.98 each, or is that for both of them?"

Sportswriter **Joe McGuff:**

> "It's been so hot in Kansas City this summer the artificial turf at Royals Stadium is beginning to die."

Former motorcycle daredevil **Evel Knievel:**

> "I think I will be one of the world's best-known painters in five years. I'd like to see Picasso or Da Vinci paint Indians the way I do."

Rick Abramson, *concessionaire at Milwaukee County Stadium, during the baseball strike:*

> "The beer will stay cold, we're putting it in frozen storage."

Sports fan **John Boles,** *talking about the NFL's Denver Broncos who play their home games near the Boulder Dam:*

> "The Broncos are the best team in the NFL by a dam site."

Montreal mayor **Jean Drapeau,** *before the 1976 Olympics:*

> "These games can no more put the taxpayers in debt than a man can have a baby."

Philadelphia Spectrum PA announcer **Dave Zinkoff:**

> "A reminder, fans, if you smoke, don't exhale."

Yogi Berra, *when asked by a BBC interviewer when the game of baseball began:*

"Eighteen something, wasn't it?"

Sports fan **Lauren Holmes:**

"The best way to watch a baseball game on television is to listen to it on the radio."

University of Wisconsin students, late in a victory which moved their team out of the Big Ten basement:

"We're No. 9!"

Sportswriter **Dan Daniel,** *who considered New York the only city in which to live:*

"Once you leave New York, it's all Bridgeport."

Anonymous:

"Anyone who says anything is possible has never tried to dribble a football."

Yankees manager **Yogi Berra,** *when asked by a reporter if he had decided on his starting line-up:*

"Not that I know of."

Windsor sportswriter **Matt Dennis,** *late in a 22-inning marathon at Tiger Stadium in Detroit:*

"I've got to leave. My visa just expired."

Pastor **Todd O'Leary** *of St. Francis de Sales Church in Tuscon, Ariz., following Notre Dame's 20-3 loss to Southern California at the Los Angeles Coliseum:*

"History has shown us once again that it is very dangerous for Christians to enter the Coliseum."

Washington State sports publicist **Oliver Pierce,** *after the Cougars were awarded one forfeit victory in 1977 and another two in 1978 because their opponents were guilty of rule violations:*

"At the rate we're going, we'll soon get a retroactive Bowl game."

Yogi Berra, *at a testimonial dinner for himself:*

"I want to thank everyone who made this day necessary."

YOGI BERRA, WHEN ASKED AT SPRING TRAINING WHAT SIZE OF HAT HE WANTED:

PSSST

HOT AIR

"I DON'T KNOW. I'M NOT IN SHAPE YET."

COME AGAIN? SAY WHAT?

Rodeo star **J.C. Trujillo:**
"Rodeoing is as American as apple pie, Chevrolet and Winston cigarettes."

Sportswriter **Tom Barnidge,** *on the large number of bowl games:*
"There are far too many bowl games. It's just a matter of time before they play a Tidy Bowl in Flushing Meadows."

A Chicago cab driver, when his customer asked to be driven to Comiskey Park:
"Comiskey Park? Is that a suburb or something?"

Baltimore manager **Earl Weaver,** *on how to keep the Orioles in first place:*
"In order to do what we've done, we have to keep doing what we've done in the past."

Writer **George Plimpton:**
"I have a theory. The larger the ball, the less the writing about the sport. There are superb books about golf, very good books about baseball, not many good books about football and very few good books about basketball. There are no books about beachballs."

Seattle mayor **Charles Moyer,** *upset after Washington Bullets coach Dick Motta made some unkind comments about the SuperSonics:*
"The man is 'persona non Motta' in Seattle."

Tom Underwood, *after he was traded to the Toronto Blue Jays:*
"They speak American up there, don't they? It's not like Montreal, is it?"

Patrick Koloski, *the director of the New Orleans sanitation department, after his city had hosted a Super Bowl game:*
"If you measure it in terms of the garbage that was left behind, it was a successful event."

Pittsburgh Steelers quarterback **Terry Bradshaw,** *talking about a less-than-memorable game during his career:*
"One time we had 10 turnovers in one game — seven fumbles and four interceptions."

258

One minor hockey executive, to another:
"Now look, be serious. This minor hockey ain't kid stuff."

Mickey Rivers, *on a cold day in Milwaukee:*
"What's the wind-shield factor?"

Yogi Berra:
"Don't imitate him if you can't copy him."

Psychologist **Michael Mahoney:**
"Thinking may be very helpful when an athlete first starts playing but later on it just interferes."

Little league baseball player, to teammate:
"What do you do when the coach signals you to steal third and your mom signals you to stay on second?"

Pittsburgh Penguins spokesman **Terry Schiffhauer,** *when asked where the team got its new uniforms:*
"From the Boston Bruins' pro shop at the Boston Garden."

Buffalo Bills coach **Hank Bullough,** *after a game in which his team gave up a 96-yard touchdown pass:*
"That play took the sails right out of our wind."

Len Barker's *92-year-old grandmother, after Barker pitched a perfect game for the Cleveland Indians against the Toronto Blue Jays:*
"I'm very proud of him but I hope he does better the next time."

University of Maryland basketball coach **Lefty Driesell:**
"I'm not really stupid. I just talk stupid."

Philadelphia Phillies pitcher **Tug McGraw,** *when asked why he was driving a 1954 Buick:*
"I like it because it plays old music."

International Olympic Committee president **Juan Antonio Samaranch,** *commenting on his administrative assistant Monique Berlioux of France:*
"Madame Berlioux is my right-hand man."

259

COME AGAIN? SAY WHAT?

New York Mets pitcher **Craig Swan,** *talking about his ambition to sail around the world:*

"It could take up to three years to make the trip, so I don't think I'll be able to do it during the season."

North Carolina State basketball player **Chuck Nevitt:**

"My sister is expecting a baby and I don't know if I'm going to be an aunt or an uncle."

Former major league manager **Frank Lucchesi,** *talking about drug use in baseball:*

"What are the players supposed to take, those illegal amphibians?"

Anonymous San Francisco Giants fan:

"Both Michael Jackson and the Giants wear gloves on their left hands for no apparent reason."

Physical fitness expert **Jack LaLanne:**

"I can't die, it would ruin my image. I can't even afford to have a fat dog."

Yogi Berra, *to a TV reporter just before the interview began:*

"If you ask me something I don't know, I'm not going to answer."

Croquet champion **Don Oberg,** *describing his approach to the game:*

"You need perseverance, pride, fortitude and a will to win. My teeth are snarling out there on that course. Everybody's my enemy when I get out there. There's just no fooling around."

Pitcher **Jeff Byrd,** *when told that he had been drafted by the Toronto Blue Jays:*

"I don't know what you're talking about. I play professional baseball."

An official of the Milwaukee Labor Council, after the Brewers announced plans to sell a Minnesota-made beer at their home games:

"We're not happy. We think it's an embarrassment to bring a foreign beer to County Stadium."

Philadelphia 76ers centre **Darryl Dawkins:**
> "When it comes to shooting, I just keep on shooting."

Yogi Berra, *during a spring training workout:*
> "Okay guys, pair off in threes."

Michael Ray Richardson *of the New Jersey Nets, during a team slump:*
> "We're on our way down and the sky's the limit."

Olympic figure skater **Elaine Zayak,** *on her limited education:*
> "I only went to high school. I mean, I thought the Hunchback of Notre Dame was a football player."

Chicago Bulls guard **Michael Jordan,** *after scoring 32 points in a game in which the Boston Celtics were without defensive ace Dennis Johnson:*
> "I took advantage of the absence of his presence."

Soccer player **Bernie James,** *on his game-day preparation:*
> "I make sure I don't have a routine. Of course, making sure I don't have a routine is actually a routine. Know what I mean?"

Edgar Jones *of the Cleveland Cavaliers:*
> "You can say so much about so many things so often. But if you do, you'll be saying nothing about anything all of the time."

Former Chicago Cubs great **Ernie Banks,** *on the popularity of baseball:*
> "People come to baseball games to study the quantitative method of optimum decision-making under conditions of uncertainty. It ameliorates the classic polarization between the self-motivated individual and the collective ideology."

Arkansas football coach **Lou Holtz,** *on graduating kicker Steve Little:*
> "We won't miss him unless we have to punt or try a field goal next year."

Baseball pitcher **Satchell Paige,** *who shied away from media coverage:*

"I want to be the onliest man in the United States that nobody knows nothing about."

Kansas City Royals pitcher **Dan Quisenberry:**

"I don't want to know my statistics, because I think I'm better if I don't think about how good I am."

New Orleans Saints running back **George Rogers,** *on his goal for an upcoming season:*

"I want to rush for 1,500 or 2,000 yards, whichever comes first."

A cheerleading prospect for the Texas Rangers, when asked if she had ever seen a major league baseball game:

"No, but I've seen the Texas Rangers play a few times."

Hamilton Tiger-Cats coach **George Dickson,** *talking about one of his players:*

"His future is all ahead of him."

Tiger Williams *of the Los Angeles Kings, explaining his check on Winnipeg's Randy Carlyle:*

"What transpired out there is that Randy Carlyle was posing for a shampoo commercial with all that beautiful blond hair of his."

Indianapolis Colts head coach **Ron Meyer,** *explaining how a new coach gets to know his players:*

"You ever see two stray dogs meet each other? They look at each other and sniff around. Well, that's the way a new coach and a team approach each other."

Yogi Berra:

"I really didn't say everything I said."

CHAPTER 23

A LITTLE DEEPER

"He's a better person than he is a hockey player."

So far in "Hot Air" you have laughed at sports people and you have laughed with sports people. Don't think, however, that these people are only flippant and frivolous.

Sports provide the people who take part with great opportunities for growth, learning and wisdom. You will experience some of that in this chapter. You will discover lifestyles, values and philosophies of utmost importance. You will hear the athletes and coaches talk about commitment, loyalty, courage, dependability, class and spiritual faith. You will hear them share their thoughts on dignity, dedication, enthusiasm, effort, trust and character. You will be challenged to always give your best in the pursuit of excellence, to dig deep within yourself in times of adversity, to accept your wins and losses in life with equal grace and to appreciate those things in this world which are truly meaningful.

Vince Lombardi:

"The quality of a man's life is in direct proportion to his commitment to excellence, regardless of his chosen field or endeavor. It's a reality of life that men are competitive and the most competitive games draw the most competitive men. That's why they're there — to compete. They know the rules and the objectives when they get in the game. The objective is to win — fairly, squarely, decently, by the rules — but to win. And in truth, I've never known a man worth his salt who in the long run, deep down in his heart, didn't appreciate the grind, the discipline. There is something in good men that really yearns for discipline and the harsh reality of head-to-head combat. I don't say these things because I believe in the 'brute' nature of man or that man must be brutalized to be combative. I believe in God and I believe in human decency. But I firmly believe that any man's finest hour — his greatest fulfilment to all he holds dear — is that moment when he has worked his heart out in a good cause and he lies exhausted on the field of battle, victorious."

Chicago Cubs great **Ernie Banks:**

"If I failed at something, it meant I learned something, so that was good."

Anonymous advice:

"Every great athlete looks inside himself in a clutch situation."

Houston Oilers coach **Bum Phillips,** *talking about running back Earl Campbell:*

"Earl may not be in a class by himself but it doesn't take long to call the roll."

Peterborough Petes coach **Gary Green:**

"Rationalization after a loss is a sure route to failure. Hard work is the key to success."

Jesse Owens, *following his victories at the 1936 Berlin Olympics:*

"When I came back, after all the stories about Hitler and his snub, I came back to my native country and I couldn't ride in the front of the bus. I had to go to the back door. I couldn't live where I wanted. I wasn't invited up to shake hands with Hitler but I wasn't invited to the White House to shake hands with the president either. Joe Louis and I were the first modern national sports figures who were black. But neither of us could do national advertising because the South wouldn't buy it. That was the social stigma we lived under."

Los Angeles Rams quarterback **Pat Haden:**

"Most people my age grew up with a tremendous social conscience because of Vietnam. And when you think about things like that, football doesn't really mean anything. In the universal sense, it's just not that important, and it shouldn't be."

Anonymous:

"There's only one thing worse than not doing your best. That's being the only one who knows."

Knute Rockne:

"When the going gets tough, the tough get going."

Former basketball great **Elvin Hayes:**

> "I was always afraid of failure. Every night, when I went out onto the court, I didn't want failure to catch me."

Chicago Bears running back **Walter Payton,** *when asked to compare himself with some of the greatest players in NFL history:*

> "Trying to compare running backs is like trying to draw the wind."

North Carolina State basketball coach **Jim Valvano:**

> "Motivation is three things — being enthusiastic, having a dream and working your butt off."

Doug Hargreaves, *head coach of the Queen's University Golden Gaels:*

> "I coach people, not football."

University of Alabama football coach **Bear Bryant:**

> "We've been able to do more with the ordinary player here than they can at other places because we never want the ordinary player to know he's ordinary. Our greatest teams usually had three or four great players and a whole lot of average ones who didn't know they were average."

Anonymous:

> "Nobody has ever learned anything from winning. Defeats are the real teachers."

Notre Dame coach **Gerry Faust:**

> "A football team is no stronger than its student body."

Sportswriter **Art Spander:**

> "Some sports people are so concerned about the destination they can't enjoy the journey."

NFL running back **Archie Griffin,** *talking about his size:*

> "It's not the size of the dog in the fight, it's the size of the fight in the dog."

Boxer **Joe Frazier:**

> "Life is wonderful, man. There's just nothin' better than livin'."

Johnny Miller, *comparing his career to that of Jack Nicklaus:*

"When I got to the top of the mountain in 1974 and 1975, I stopped to admire the view. Whenever Jack reached the top of a mountain, he started looking for another mountain."

Marathon runner **Stan Cottrell:**

"I never wanted to be average, because when you are average you are just as far from the top as you are from the bottom."

Anonymous:

"Never assume you are incapable of executing a particular skill. Confidence is often akin to performance."

U. S. President **Jimmy Carter,** *about Jesse Owens:*

"Perhaps no athlete better symbolized the human struggle against tyranny, poverty and racial bigotry."

M.L. Carr *of the Boston Celtics, talking about general manager Red Auerbach's approach to racial problems on the team:*

"We don't have black players or white players. We have Celtic green players."

Baron de Coubertin, *the founder of the modern Olympics:*

"The Olympic movement tends to gather in radiant splendor all the principles that work towards man's perfection."

New York Knicks great **Spencer Haywood:**

"Some people call me a superstar but I'll tell you who is really a superstar. It's a man or woman raising kids on a limited income and teaching them good values. That's who society should call a superstar."

Jim Valvano:

"I grew up with the greatest gift a person can have — a good family."

Kansas City Kings coach **Cotton Fitzsimmons:**

"Never underestimate the power of positive thinking. If you're a positive thinker, you are an automatic motivator."

Lou Holtz:

"Happiness is nothing more than a poor memory."

California Angels manager **Gene Mauch,** *on praise:*

"Praise is like perfume. It's nice to smell once in a while but if you swallow it, you'll get sick."

Olympic pole vaulting champion **Bob Richards:**

"Regardless of what you do in life, you have to work to be the best you can be."

Hockey great **Gordie Howe:**

"A mistake is not a mistake until it's made the second time."

University of Indiana basketball coach **Bobby Knight:**

"Leaders don't negotiate either values or goals."

Edmonton Oilers defenceman **Paul Coffey,** *when asked to describe teammate Wayne Gretzky:*

"He's a better person than he is a hockey player. That's what makes him so good."

Anonymous:

"Regardless of the sport, always be kind to beginners. Remember, you were once one yourself."

Mike Eruzione, *the captain of the U.S. hockey team which won a gold medal at the Lake Placid Olympics:*

"Hero? Vietnam vets are heroes. The guys who tried to rescue our hostages in Iran are heroes. I'm just a hockey player."

Toronto Maple Leafs forward **Wendel Clark:**

"You work hard when you get the opportunity to work hard. That way you'll never let yourself or other people down."

Houston Oilers running back **Earl Campbell,** *on motivation:*

"I understand that Vince Lombardi was a great motivator but he couldn't teach my momma anything."

Sportswriter **Andy O'Brien:**

"Championship is a state of mind."

Philadelphia Flyers assistant coach **Bernie Parent,** *during the memorial service for Pelle Lindbergh:*

"It doesn't matter how dark the sky looks, if you have faith, the sun will come out."

Booker T. Washington:

"Success is to be measured, not so much by the position one has reached in life but by the obstacles one has overcome while trying to succeed."

Western Mustangs football coach **Darwin Semotiuk:**

"In the game of sport as in the game of life, you have to be able to handle your victories with class but you have to be able to handle your setbacks with class as well."

Philadelphia Flyers coach **Fred Shero:**

"Failure is never fatal."

U. S. President **Theodore Roosevelt:**

"Far greater it is to dare mighty things, to win glorious triumphs even though checkered by failure, than to abide with those poor spirits who neither enjoy much nor suffer much, neither know winning nor defeat."

Bill Copeland:

"You must have a goal in life. If you don't have a goal in life, you can spend your time running up and down the field and never scoring."

Detroit Red Wings general manager **Jim Devellano:**

"I find that living patience is a little tougher than talking about it."

Anonymous:

"Practise faithfully until the time arrives when you realize you still have much to learn. That moment will be your soul's awakening."

Billie Jean King:

"Girls are taught in subtle ways not to be competitive. But there's nothing wrong with a female being competitive. All it means is that you're trying to do your best."

Sportscaster **Dick Schaap:**

"Part of the problem in sports is that a lot of us take it a little too seriously."

Brooklyn Dodgers general manager **Branch Rickey:**

"Luck is the residue of design."

Baseball broadcaster **Vin Scully:**

"It's a mere moment in a man's life between an all-star game and an oldtimers game."

Toronto sportscaster **Bill Stephenson:**

"Remember, you don't have to play a sport to be a good one."

Sports journalist **Larry King:**

"I love that moment of solitude right before any sporting event begins."

Chicago Cubs shortstop **Ernie Banks:**

"If we don't win today, we'll win tomorrow. If we don't win this season, we'll win next season."

Baseball great **Hank Aaron,** *talking about Jackie Robinson and Roy Campanella:*

"They proved to the world that a man's ability is limited only by his lack of opportunity."

Anonymous:

"It is amazing how much can be accomplished when nobody is worrying about who gets the credit."

Baseball great **Gil Hodges,** *speaking to a rookie:*

"You have talent but a lot of young players have talent. Dedication and hard work will decide whether you have success."

Plaque in the Pittsburgh Pirates locker room, dedicated to the late Bob Moose:

"A great competitor who had desire, confidence, class and style but above all the ability to be color-blind when it came to people from origins other than his own."

Sportscaster **Tory Gregg:**

"You always win if you lose with a smile."

Mickey Rivers:

"Ain't no sense worrying about the things you got no control over, 'cause if you got no control over 'em, ain't no sense worrying about 'em."

Mark 'The Bird' Fidrych:

"I've known the top and I've known the bottom and how many guys ever get to say that? I figure it's made a better person out of me."

Anonymous:

"Is it not hypocritical to infuse children with the desire to succeed and then tell them the result of a game is immaterial? Problems arise not so much from winning or losing but in the response to winning and losing."

Montreal Expos shortstop **Chris Speier,** *putting baseball into perspective:*

"I make an error that costs us a game and riding the bus back to the hotel I see somebody eating out of a garbage can. I've got troubles?"

New York Yankees outfielder **Bobby Murcer,** *on his happy disposition:*

"Life is too short to be going around grumpy and depressed."

Jesse Owens, *following his victories in the 1936 Berlin Olympics:*

"I saw Hitler in his box but to me he was just another head of state. I wasn't running against Hitler, I was running against the world."

New York Yankees great **Lou Gehrig,** *despite his imminent death:*

"I consider myself the luckiest man on the face of the earth."

NFL great **Gale Sayers:**

"My God is first, my family and friends are second, I am third."

Boston Red Sox great **Carl Yastrzemski,** *explaining his fascination with baseball:*

> "I love the one-on-one. You're alone. No one can help you. No one can help the other guy. Baseball is a great character-builder. You can't make excuses. It has humbled me many times."

Pittsburgh Steelers running back **Rocky Bleier:**

> "When I retire, it won't be the practices and training camps I'll miss. It will be the competition and the guys. Teams have special relationships and when you're on the outside, you can never be a member of the team again."

Dallas Cowboys running back **Tony Dorsett:**

> "The guy who responds to pressure is the true champion."

Bobby Clarke:

> "Championships are the ultimate for any athlete but you don't really need championships to be fulfilled. The satisfaction of knowing that you're doing the best you can at your job is the most important. Then you can look at yourself in the mirror and be content."

TV commentator **Pepper Rodgers:**

> "Football coaches like to talk about building character. They don't build character. They eliminate those who don't have it."

San Francisco columnist **Art Spander:**

> "Baseball is as much meant to be absorbed as it is to be observed."

Seattle Seahawks coach **Chuck Knox:**

> "In this league, you have to instill a will to win and a will to prepare — two entirely different things and the true test of a coach."

University of Miami football coach **Howard Schnellenberger,** *on the difference between involvement and commitment:*

> "When you're eating ham and eggs, the chicken that laid the eggs was involved, the pig that provided the ham was totally committed."

Essayist **Gilbert Sorrentino:**

"Baseball is a pure game of continual action, which is not to be confused with continual movement."

Detroit Lions coach **Monte Clark,** *remembering the death of his three-year-old daughter to leukemia:*

"You want to quit football, you want to quit everything. But you soon realize that you can't do that."

Green Bay Packers coach **Bart Starr:**

"There are going to be times during the careers of coaches and players — several times — when you play well and you're still defeated. You have nothing to be ashamed of at a time like that."

Jim Valvano, *putting college basketball into perspective:*

"For 40 minutes, the most important thing in the world is basketball. When it's over, we have to understand the relative unimportance of what we just did, the unimportance to the world and to the rest of our lives. If basketball becomes the end-all, there are going to be a lot of sad stories."

University of Windsor football coach **Gino Fracas:**

"The 'ABC' of sports is 'adversity builds character.' "

Bum Phillips:

"An expert is an ordinary fella away from home."

Sports journalist **Larry King:**

"There is no more unimportantly important thing on this planet than sports."

Stanford football coach **Rod Dowhower:**

"When loyalties go by the wayside, ideals go by the wayside."

John Nooney, *describing a leader:*

"A leader is one who has a plan, one who keeps heading towards a goal and a purpose. He has the enthusiasm to keep moving forward in such a way that others gladly go with him."

Bear Bryant:

> "Football does not build character. But if an athlete comes to us with character, we can develop it."

University of Nebraska football coach **Tom Osborne:**

> "It's easy to get a false impression of your own importance when you win. You need to realize how temporary and transitory that importance is."

Vince Lombardi:

> "Show me a coach who doesn't stress fundamentals and I'll show you a loser."

Anonymous:

> "A good sport is always a winner."

Baseball great **Joe Morgan:**

> "As long as I do my best, I'll never have to walk off the field with my head down."

Sportswriter **Red Smith,** *writing about colleague Grantland Rice:*

> "He wrote of men he loved and deeds he admired and never knew how much bigger he was than his finest hero."

Writer **Lawrence S. Ritter:**

> "As a symbol of joy and loyalty, a shared illusion that links generation to generation, baseball has grown from the fragile roots of trust, faith, allegiance and make-believe that bind owners, players and fans in a common fate. The strongest thing baseball has going for it today is its yesterdays."

Canadian hero **Terry Fox:**

> "Somewhere the hurting must stop."

San Francisco columnist **Art Spander:**

> "Baseball is a game of numbers and nuances in which time is subordinate to circumstance."

Pat Haden, *on defeat:*

> "It's something we all have to learn to accept. It's part of playing the game. Nobody wins all the time. Dignity is knowing how to deal with both victory and defeat."

Canadian humorist **Stephen Leacock:**

> "I am a great believer in luck and I find that the harder I work, the more I have of it."

Jesse Owens, *talking about the benefits of athletics to racial and political problems:*

> "In due time, there will be a better peace and better feeling among men because of sports."

Canadian Member of Parliamant **Gus McFarlane,** *during a debate in the House of Commons:*

> "Athletics is poetry in motion."

Author **Roger Kahn:**

> "To age with dignity and with courage cuts close to what it takes to be a man."

Anonymous:

> "Baseball enables the generations to talk to each other. At World Series time, conversations are more eloquent. Tradition steps into the batter's box. Mythology and history are inseparable."

Don K. Shayne:

> "Would the boy you were be proud of the man you are?"

Sportswriter **Red Smith:**

> "Ninety feet between bases is the closest man has come to perfection."

Penn State football coach **Joe Paterno:**

> "A team is either getting better or it's getting worse. It can't stay the same."

Chicago Blackhawks centre **Stan Mikita:**

> "If you play to win as I do, the game never ends."

San Francisco Giants manager **Roger Craig:**

> "Losing was a tremendous influence in shaping my pitching philosophy. I learned the value of being competitive, regardless of the circumstances."

Woody Hayes:

"Winning is the most honorable thing a man can do."

Bernie Parent, *at the memorial service for Philadelphia goaltender Pelle Lindbergh:*

"When death defeats greatness, we mourn. When death defeats youth, we mourn even more."

Jack Nicklaus:

"A large part of winning comes from true desire."

Bart Starr, *talking about Vince Lombardi:*

"He taught me that winning is not everything but the effort to win is."

Muhammad Ali:

"Only losers lose."

Anonymous:

"If you count winning and fun as two possible rewards of playing, losing and fun get you one out of two."

Philadelphia Eagles coach **Dick Vermeil,** *on his dedication to the game:*

"If you don't invest very much, then defeat doesn't hurt very much and winning isn't very exciting."

Jim Valvano:

"We ask our young people to be three things. We ask them to be the best students they can possibly be, the best athletes they can possibly be and the best people they can possibly be. If we can accomplish those three goals, then we're going to be successful regardless of the outcomes of a few basketball games."

Howard Cosell:

"One of the hardest lessons in life is not to take seriously what anyone says in anger."

Anonymous:

"All of us lose occasionally but we're never beaten until we quit."